COLLECTIONS

Practice Book
Grade 1

Open Doors

You're Invited

Bright Ideas

Harcourt

Orlando   Boston   Dallas   Chicago   San Diego

Visit *The Learning Site!*
www.harcourtschool.com

Contents

Harcourt

Table of Contents **3**

Contents

YOU'RE INVITED

Harcourt

Contents

BRIGHT IDEAS

Harcourt

Contents

Harcourt

Open
Doors

Name _____

► **Say the name of the picture. Write m if the word begins with the /m/ sound.**

1.

_____

- - - - - - - - - - - - -

_____

2.

_____

- - - - - - - - - - - - -

_____

3.

_____

- - - - - - - - - - - - -

_____

4.

_____

- - - - - - - - - - - - -

_____

5.

_____

- - - - - - - - - - - - -

_____

6.

_____

- - - - - - - - - - - - -

_____

TRY THIS Use a crayon to print a big m. Use other colors to trace around the m. Say "M-M-M-M" as you work.

SCHOOL-HOME CONNECTION Ask your child to name the pictures that begin with the sound m. Think of more words that begin with the same sound.

Harcourt

▶ **Say a sentence to tell what happens in each picture.**

1.

2.

3.

4.

SCHOOL-HOME CONNECTION With your child say
a few short sentences. Discuss that a sentence tells
a complete thought.

Name _____

▶ **Finish each sentence. Write <u>I</u> and <u>a</u>.**

1. <u>I</u> 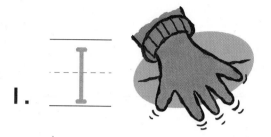 <u>a</u>  .

2. _____  _____  .

3. _____  _____  .

4. _____ 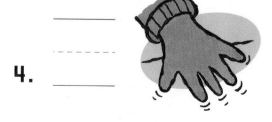 _____  .

SCHOOL-HOME CONNECTION Ask your child to tell you about the sentences he or she completed on this page. Have your child point to the word *I* and then to the word *a*.

Harcourt

Name _____

▶ **Say the name of each picture. Circle the picture if the name has the /a/ sound.**

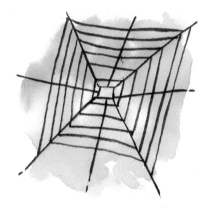

Harcourt

SCHOOL-HOME CONNECTION Ask your child to name the pictures whose names have short vowel *a*. Find at least one more object in the house whose name has the short *a* sound.

Open Doors Theme 1
Lesson 2

11

▶ **Say the name of the picture. Write s̲ on the line if the name begins with the /s/ sound.**

1.

s

2.

3.

4.

5.

6.

SCHOOL-HOME CONNECTION Make up an "s song" by singing words that begin with the sound s to a tune your child knows.

Name _____

▶ **Write the word that completes each sentence.**

here   is
_____

1. Where _____ ?

Where   Is
_____

2. _____ is  ?

Where   Is
_____

3. _____ is ?

Is   Here
_____

4. _____ I am!

TRY THIS Where else could Rabbit hide? Draw a picture to show your idea.

 SCHOOL-HOME CONNECTION With your child, take turns asking and answering questions. Begin questions with the word *where*. Begin answers with the word *here*.

Open Doors Theme 1
Lesson 4

13

Harcourt

Name _____

Phonics

Short Vowel: /a/a;
Consonants: /s/s,
/m/m

▶ Say the name of the picture. Write **m** or **s** to show the beginning sound. Draw a circle around the pictures that show animals.

1.  _____

2.  _____

3.  _____

4. 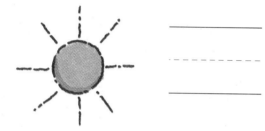 _____

▶ Say the name of the picture. Write **a** if the name has the sound /a/. Draw a circle around the pictures that show animals.

5. 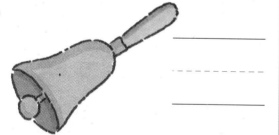 _____

6.  _____

7.  _____

8.  _____

SCHOOL-HOME CONNECTION Have your child print s, a, and m on scrap paper. Say sit, men, cat, and Sam. Stop after each word and have your child point to the letter that stands for the sound they hear at the beginning of each word.

Harcourt

Name _____

▶ **Think about the story. Draw Sam.**
Show what Sam was doing at the end of
the story.

 TRY THIS What do you think Sam's mother did when she found him? Draw a picture to show your idea.

SCHOOL-HOME CONNECTION Ask your child to tell you about the story *Where Is Sam?* Ask them who Sam is and what he did.

Open Doors Theme 1
Lesson 4 **15**

Name _____

▶ **Name each picture. If the name rhymes with Sam, write am.**

1.

_____

- - - - - - - - - -

_____

2.

_____

- - - - - - - - - -

_____

3.

_____

- - - - - - - - - -

_____

4.

_____

- - - - - - - - - -

_____

5.

_____

- - - - - - - - - -

_____

6.

_____

- - - - - - - - - -

_____

▶ **Draw a picture of yourself. Then finish the sentence.**

_____

- - - - - - - - - - - - - -

I am _____.

SCHOOL-HOME CONNECTION Ask your child to name the pictures that end with the same sounds you can hear at the end of *Sam*. Together, make up a short poem with two of the words.

Harcourt

► Say the name of the picture. Write <u>t</u> if the name begins or ends with the /t/ sound.

1.

_____

- - - - - - - - - - -

_____

2.

_____

- - - - - - - - - - -

_____

3.

_____

- - - - - - - - - - -

_____

4.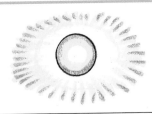

_____

- - - - - - - - - - -

_____

5.

_____

- - - - - - - - - - -

_____

6.

_____

- - - - - - - - - - -

_____

TRY THIS Draw a picture of a teddy bear. Draw a cap on the teddy bear and write <u>T</u> on it. Give your teddy bear a name that begins with <u>T</u>.

SCHOOL-HOME CONNECTION Find ten things in your house whose names begin with the sound t stands for.

Open Doors Theme 1
Lesson 6

17

Harcourt

Name _____

▶ **Circle each word group that is a sentence. Then write each sentence. Draw a picture to go with your sentences.**

is where   Here I am.   Sam Sam

Where is Sam?   is where   Sam is here.

1. _____

2. _____

3. _____

Open Doors Theme 1
Lesson 6

SCHOOL-HOME CONNECTION Let your child point out sentences on this page or in a book. Ask where one sentence ends and the next sentence begins.

Harcourt

Name _____

▶ **Write the word that best completes each sentence.**

look   that

1. Where is _____ ?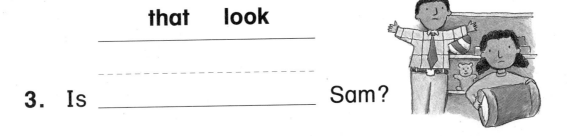

That   Look

2. _____ here.

that   look

3. Is _____ Sam?

Look   That

4. _____ ! Here is that .

TRY THIS Write a sentence. Use the words <u>look</u> and <u>that</u>. Draw a picture to go with your sentence.

SCHOOL-HOME CONNECTION Play a guessing game like "I Spy" with your child. Take turns giving clues and guessing the answer.

Open Doors Theme 1
Lesson 7

19

Harcourt

Name _____

Phonics
Short Vowel: /a/a
Consonants: /t/t,
/m/m

▶ **Say the name of the picture. Write t̲ or m̲ to show the beginning sound.**

1. _____

2. _____

3. _____

4. _____

▶ **Say the name of the picture. Write a̲ if the name has the /a/ sound.**

5. _____

6. _____

7. _____

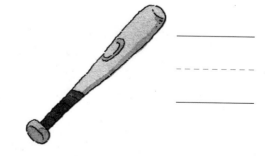

8. _____

SCHOOL-HOME CONNECTION Have your child print t, a, and m on scrap paper. Say at, am, and mat. Have your child use the letters to spell each word.

Harcourt

Name _____

▶ **Finish each picture. Show where Sam sat first, next, and last.**

First

Next

Last

SCHOOL-HOME CONNECTION Ask your child to
tell you where the mouse sat in the story.

Open Doors Theme 1
Lesson 7   **21**

Harcourt

Name _____

▶ **Say the name of the picture. Write c if the name of the picture begins with /k/.**

1.

___ ___
___ C ___

2.

___ ___
___ ___

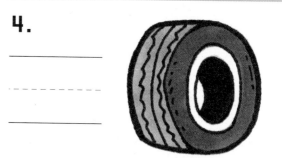

3.

___ ___
___ ___

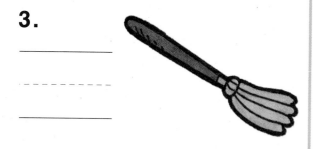

4.

___ ___
___ ___

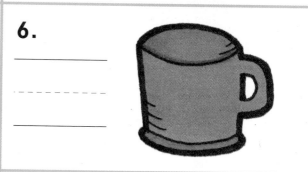

5.

___ ___
___ ___

6.

___ ___
___ ___

7.

___ ___
___ ___

8.

___ ___
___ ___

TRY THIS Write your own sentence about something you need. Draw a picture to go with your sentence.

 SCHOOL-HOME CONNECTION Look out the window. Count the number of cars you see.

Harcourt

Name _____

▶ **Write the word that best completes each sentence.**

me   come
_____

- -

1. Look at _____!

---

me   come
_____

- -

2. Here I _____. I am a cat.

Me   Come
_____

- -

3. _____ here.

---

me   come
_____

- -

4. Look at _____. I am Sam.

TRY THIS Write this sentence: Look at me! Draw a picture to go with your sentence.

SCHOOL-HOME CONNECTION Talk with your child about friends and family members who visit your home. Encourage your child to name the people who visit.

Name _____

▶ **Name each picture. Circle the pictures whose names begin with /k/. Then write the letter c.**

1.

_____

C

2.

_____

3.

_____

4.

_____

5.

_____

6.

_____

▶ **Read the words in the box. Write each word under the correct picture.**

mat	cat

7.

_____

8.

_____

Open Doors Theme 1
Lesson 9

SCHOOL-HOME CONNECTION Write the word *cat*, and let your child read the word to you. Together, think of other words that begin with the same sound you hear at the beginning of *cat*.

Harcourt

Name _____

▶ **Think about the story. Draw pictures of the two main characters. Write the characters' names under your pictures. Now draw a picture to show the story ending.**

_____   _____

- - - - - - - - - - - -   - - - - - - - - - - - -

_____   _____

SCHOOL-HOME CONNECTION Ask your child about the story *Come Here, Cat.* What game does Sam try to play? Ask him or her how Cat feels about the game.

Open Doors Theme 1
Lesson 9   **25**

Name _____

▶ **Name each picture. If the name rhymes with __Sam__, write __am__. If the name rhymes with __cat__, write __at__.**

1.

_____

- - - - - - - - - - -

_____

2.

_____

- - - - - - - - - - -

_____

3.

_____

- - - - - - - - - - -

_____

4.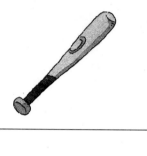

_____

- - - - - - - - - - -

_____

5.

_____

- - - - - - - - - - -

_____

6.

_____

- - - - - - - - - - -

_____

Open Doors Theme 1
Lesson 10

SCHOOL-HOME CONNECTION Say the tongue twister *Hide the ham in Heidi's hat.* Ask your child which word ends with *–am* and which word ends with *–at.* Then practice saying the tongue twister together, as fast as you can.

Harcourt

Name _____

▶ **Name each picture. Write the letter p if the name begins with p.**

1.
_____
- - - - - - -
p
_____

2.
_____
- - - - - - -
_____

3.
_____
- - - - - - -
_____

4.
_____
- - - - - - -
_____

5.
_____
- - - - - - -
_____

6.
_____
- - - - - - -
_____

7.
_____
- - - - - - -
_____

8.
_____
- - - - - - -
_____

9.
_____
- - - - - - -
_____

TRY THIS Draw a picture of something whose name begins with p. Color it purple or pink even if it looks silly.

SCHOOL-HOME CONNECTION Hunt through the house for things that are purple or pink.

Open Doors Theme 1
Lesson 11

27

Harcourt

Name _____

▶ **Silly Sam's words are all mixed up.**
Write the words in order.

1. I Sam. am

_____

- - - - - - - - - - - - - - - - - - - -

_____

2. sat I here.

_____

_____

3. here. sat Matt

_____

- - - - - - - - - - - - - - - - - - - -

_____

4. cat here. A sat

_____

- - - - - - - - - - - - - - - - - - - -

_____

TRY THIS Draw a picture of yourself. Make up a sentence about it. Say your words in order.

SCHOOL-HOME CONNECTION Say a short sentence. Mix up the order of two words in your sentence. Ask your child to say the sentence with the words in the right order.

Harcourt

Name _____

▶ **Write the word that completes each sentence.**

has   the

_____

- - - - - - - - - - - - - - - - - -

1. Where is _____  ?

has   good

_____

- - - - - - - - - - - - - - - - - -

2. Pam _____ the .

---

the   has

_____

- - - - - - - - - - - - - - - - - -

3. Here is _____ .

the   good

_____

- - - - - - - - - - - - - - - - - -

4. Mmmm! The is _____ !

 TRY THIS   Draw a picture of something you think is good.

SCHOOL-HOME CONNECTION Write the words *the, has,* and *good,* and let your child read them to you. Take turns making up sentences that use all three words.

Open Doors Theme 1
Lesson 12   **29**

Name _____

Phonics

Short Vowel: /a/a
Consonants: /p/p,
/t/t

▶ **Say the name of each picture. Color the oval pink if the name begins with /p/. Color the oval green if the name begins with /t/. Color the oval blue if the name has the /a/ sound.**

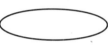

SCHOOL-HOME CONNECTION With your child, write a silly story about a pig named Pat. Have your child circle words that contain the letter p.

Harcourt

Name _____

▶ **Finish the story map. Write the word from the box that best completes each sentence. Then draw a picture about the end of the story.**

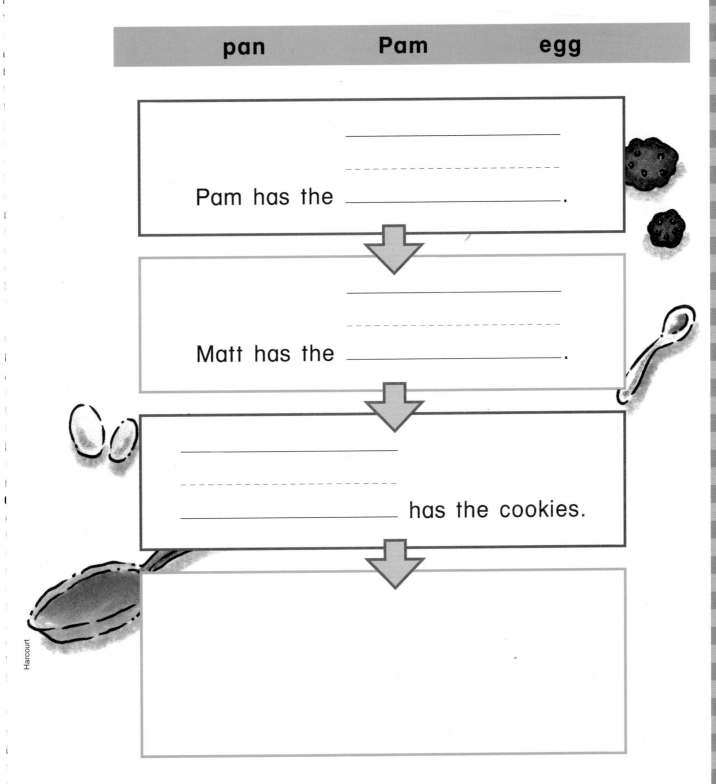

| pan | Pam | egg |

Pam has the _____.

Matt has the _____.

_____ has the cookies.

SCHOOL-HOME CONNECTION Let your child tell you about the story *Pass the Cookies*. Ask him or her who made the cookies and who ate the cookies.

Open Doors Theme 1
Lesson 12

31

▶ **Name each picture. Write the letter <u>h</u> if the name begins with the sound /h/.**

1.

h

2.

3.

4.

5.

6.

7.

8.

9.

TRY THIS Put your hand on a sheet of paper. Open your fingers and trace your hand. Draw a picture of something you are happy about.

 SCHOOL-HOME CONNECTION Ask your child to draw a picture of your home. Help him or her write your address on the picture.

Harcourt

Name _____

▶ **Look at each picture. Write the word that completes the sentence.**

    red   the

    _____

    - - - - - - - -

I. Sam has a _____ cat.

    red   too

    _____

    - - - - - - - -

2. Pat has a red cat, _____.

    egg   big

    _____

    - - - - - - - -

3. That cat is _____!

    too   me

    _____

    - - - - - - - -

4. That cat is big _____.

    has   red

    _____

    - - - - - - - -

5. Is that cat _____?

SCHOOL-HOME CONNECTION Write the word *red*, and let your child read it aloud. Then ask your child to name at least six things that are red.

Open Doors Theme 1
Lesson 14

33

Harcourt

Name _____

Phonics

Short Vowel: /a/a
Consonants: /s/s,
/h/h

▶ **Look at each picture. Write the word that best completes each sentence.**

| ham | mat | sat | has | hat |

_____

1. Here is the _____.

_____

2. Is that the _____?

_____

3. Where is the _____?

_____

4. Pam _____ the map.

_____

5. Pat _____.

SCHOOL-HOME CONNECTION Write a list of things you would pack for a trip to the beach. Have your child point out any words that contain the sounds short a, s, or h.

Harcourt

▶ **Think about the story. Circle the words that tell about the story. Draw a picture to show what happened at the end.**

Pam	Matt	Sam
Cat	red hat	big hat

SCHOOL-HOME CONNECTION Ask your child to tell you about the hats in the story. Who wore the funniest hat of all?

Open Doors Theme 1
Lesson 14   **35**

Name _____

▶ **Name each picture. If the name rhymes with tap, write ap. If the name rhymes with sat, write at.**

1.

_____

- - - - - - - - - -

_____

2.

_____

- - - - - - - - - -

_____

3.

_____

- - - - - - - - - -

_____

4.

_____

- - - - - - - - - -

_____

5.

_____

- - - - - - - - - -

_____

6.

_____

- - - - - - - - - -

_____

7.

_____

- - - - - - - - - -

_____

8.

_____

- - - - - - - - - -

_____

9.

_____

- - - - - - - - - -

_____

SCHOOL-HOME CONNECTION With your child make up a short rhyme using words that end with –at and –ap.

Harcourt

Name _____

▶ **Finish each sentence. Add <u>s</u> to the word above the line. Write that new word on the line.**

come
_____

1. Here _____ Sam.

pat
_____

2. Pam _____ Sam.

cat
_____

3. Here come the _____.

look
_____

4. Sam _____ at the cats.

meow
_____

5. The red cat _____ at Sam.

Harcourt

SCHOOL-HOME CONNECTION Write the words *hat* and *hats*.
Ask your child to tell you how the two words are different.
With your child, make up a sentence using both words.

Name _____

► **Write the word in the box that best completes each sentence.**

dad	sad	mad	had	pad

1. I am _____.

2. I am _____.

3. I _____ a cap.

4. I see the _____.

5. I see my _____.

SCHOOL-HOME CONNECTION Ask your child to read aloud the words in the box. Have him or her tell you which letter is at the end of each word. Encourage your child to name familiar objects that begin with the *d* sound.

Harcourt

Name _____

▶ **Write these telling sentences correctly.**

1. look at that

_____

- - - - - - - - - - - - - - - - - - -

_____

2. i see a cat

_____

- - - - - - - - - - - - - - - - - - -

_____

3. the cat has a hat

_____

- - - - - - - - - - - - - - - - - - -

_____

4. the cat comes

_____

- - - - - - - - - - - - - - - - - - -

_____

TRY THIS Write a telling sentence about your favorite food.

SCHOOL-HOME CONNECTION Ask your child to say a few sentences about a cat. Write the sentences. Have your child point out the capital letters and periods.

Open Doors Theme 2
Lesson 1

39

Harcourt

Name _____

▶ **Write the word that completes each sentence.**

on   see

1. I _____ a cat.

This   See

2. _____ is a good cat.

---

see   on

3. The cat is _____ me.

---

see   this

4. I _____ a hat.

TRY THIS Draw three things you can see in your classroom.

SCHOOL-HOME CONNECTION Talk about what *on* means. Ask your child to name three things that are on something in the room.

Harcourt

Name _____

Phonics
Consonants: /d/d,
/h/h
Short Vowel: /a/a

▶ **Write the word from the box that names each picture.**

| ham | hats | dad | pads | map | cats |

1. _____

2. _____

3. _____

4. _____

5. _____

6. _____

SCHOOL-HOME CONNECTION Ask your child to say some words that begin with the sound for *h*.

Open Doors Theme 2
Lesson 2   41

Harcourt

Name _____

▶ **Think about the story. Look at each
picture. If it happened in the story, color the
happy face. If it did not happen, color the sad face.**

1.

2.

3.

4.

5.

Open Doors Theme 2
Lesson 2

SCHOOL-HOME CONNECTION Encourage your child to tell you about
the circus tricks in the story *Come On, Dad*. Together, talk about some
real performing tricks you may have seen at a circus or on television.

Name _____

▶ **Name each picture. Listen for the sound in the middle of the word. Write i if you hear the sound /i/.**

1. _____	2. _____	3. _____

4. _____	5. _____	6. _____

7. _____	8. _____	9. _____

SCHOOL-HOME CONNECTION Ask your child to identify the letter that stands for the sound you hear at the beginning of the word *igloo*. Have your child practice writing that letter.

Harcourt

Name _____

▶ **Write the word that best completes each sentence.**

What   Will
_____

- - - - - - - - -

1. _____ it tip?

What   Will
_____

- - - - - - - - -

2. _____ will Pat do?

now   do
_____

- - - - - - - - -

3. Did Pat _____ that?

now   do
_____

- - - - - - - - -

4. It will tip _____!

What   Will
_____

- - - - - - - - -

5. _____ will Pat do now?

SCHOOL-HOME CONNECTION With your child, take turns making up silly questions with this beginning: *What will you do when...?*

Harcourt

Name _____

▶ **Write the words where they belong in the puzzle.**

hit	tip	pat	pit	pad

1.

2.

3.

4.

5.

1. ↓

3. ↓

2. →

4. →

5. ↓

SCHOOL-HOME CONNECTION Ask what sound your child hears in the middle of the word *sit*. Together, think of other words that have the same sound.

Open Doors Theme 2
Lesson 4

Name _____

▶ **Think about the story. Draw what happened first, next, and last.**

First

⬇

Next

⬇

Last

SCHOOL-HOME CONNECTION Ask your child to tell you the beginning, the middle, and the end of the story. Then play a game, with one player beginning a new story and the next player adding to the story.

Harcourt

Name _____

► **Look at each picture. Circle the word that completes the sentence. Then write the word.**

1. Here is _____.

Dad
Did
Mad

2. Dad _____ a mitt.

his
dad
had

3. I _____ his mitt.

mad
sit
hid

4. Dad is _____.

sat
sit
sad

5. I _____ it.

dad
did
mad

Harcourt

SCHOOL-HOME CONNECTION Ask your child to write the words *had* and *hid*. Let your child point out the letters that are the same and the letters that are different.

Name _____

▶ **Look at each picture. Circle the word that completes each sentence. Then write the word.**

1. Look _____ Tim.

it
at
pat

2. Tim is a _____ .

mat
mitt
cat

3. Tim can _____ .

sit
sat
pit

4. Tim has a _____ .

hit
hat
it

5. _____ is red.

Hit
At
It

Open Doors Theme 2
Lesson 5

SCHOOL-HOME CONNECTION Ask your child to say three
words that rhyme with *sit* and three words that rhyme with *sat*.

Harcourt

Name _____

▶ **Name each picture. Write <u>n</u> if the name begins or ends with the /n/ sound.**

1.

n

2.

3.

4.

5.

6.

7.

8.

9.

SCHOOL-HOME CONNECTION With your child, think of other words that begin with the sound you hear at the beginning of *nap*. Then let your child practice writing the letter *n*.

Open Doors Theme 2
Lesson 6

49

Harcourt

Name _____

▶ **Write these asking sentences correctly.**

1. where is the bike

_____

- -

_____

2. do you see that

_____

- -

_____

3. can Dad do that

_____

- -

_____

4. what will you do

_____

- -

_____

▶ **Read the sentences. Circle the asking sentence. Underline the telling sentence.**

Where is the cat?   **The cat is in here.**

TRY THIS What do you want to know about the bike? Write your own asking sentence. Use a capital letter and a question mark.

SCHOOL-HOME CONNECTION Help your child identify asking sentences. Write dictated sentences and have your child write the question mark for each one.

Harcourt

Name _____

▶ **Write the word that best completes each sentence.**

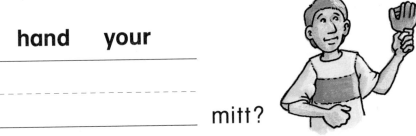

hand   your

_____

- -

1. Is this _____ mitt?

my   hand

_____

- -

2. Your _____ is too big.

not   hand

_____

- -

3. My hand is _____ big.

my   hand

_____

- -

4. It is _____ mitt.

TRY THIS Trace your hand. Write the sentence
This is my hand.

SCHOOL-HOME CONNECTION Write the word *not*, and
let your child read it to you. Then take turns making up
silly sentences or poems using the word *not*.

Open Doors Theme 2
Lesson 7   51

Harcourt

Name _____

Phonics

Short Vowel: /a/a
Consonants: /n/n,
/d/d

▶ **Look at each picture. Circle the word that completes the sentence. Then write the word.**

_____

1. I see a _____ .

mad
man
nap

_____

2. This man is my _____ .

had
did
dad

_____

3. My dad has a _____ .

can
cat
hat

_____

4. Here is the _____ .

pad
pan
pin

_____

5. My dad has a _____ .

pin
pad
nap

Open Doors Theme 2
Lesson 7

SCHOOL-HOME CONNECTION Have your child point to the word *man* on this page. Together, think of several words that rhyme with the word *man*.

Harcourt

Name _____

▶ **Think about the story. Read each sentence. If it tells about the story, color the happy face. If it does not tell about the story, color the sad face.**

1. Dan has it.

2. It is big.

3. It is not in his hand.

4. It is in a hat.

5. It is a snail.

SCHOOL-HOME CONNECTION Let your child tell you about the surprise in the story *What Is It?* Then play a game with your child, taking turns giving clues and asking, "What is it?"

Open Doors Theme 2
Lesson 7   53

Harcourt

Name _____

▶ **Name each picture. Write the word in the box that best names each picture.**

kids	sack	kit	tack	kick	pack

1.

_____

- - - - - - - - - - - -

_____

2.

_____

- - - - - - - - - - - -

_____

3.

_____

- - - - - - - - - - - -

_____

4.

_____

- - - - - - - - - - - -

_____

5.

_____

- - - - - - - - - - - -

_____

6.

_____

- - - - - - - - - - - -

_____

TRY THIS Write a word that begins or ends with the /k/ sound. Draw a picture to go with the word.

Open Doors Theme 2
Lesson 8

54

SCHOOL-HOME CONNECTION Have your child point out words that begin and end with the /k/ sound. Together, think of other words that begin or end with that sound.

Harcourt

Name _____

▶ **Write the word in the box that best completes each sentence.**

for	one	two	you

_____

1. Do _____ see the apples?

_____

2. I see _____ big apples!

_____

3. Is one apple _____ me?

_____

4. This _____ is for me.

 TRY THIS Draw a picture of two things you like. Write a sentence to go with your picture.

SCHOOL-HOME CONNECTION Write the words *one* and *two*, and let your child read them aloud. Then take turns naming things you can see one of and things you can see two of.

Open Doors Theme 2
Lesson 9

55

Harcourt

Name _____

Phonics

Short Vowel: /i/i
Consonants: /k/k,
ck, /n/n

▶ **Look at the pictures. Write the word in the box that best completes each sentence.**

kick	Nick	pack	pick

1.

_____

Kip can _____.

2.

_____

_____ can nap.

3.

_____

Pam can _____.

4.

_____

Dan can _____.

SCHOOL-HOME CONNECTION Ask your child to point out the word *kick* on this page. Encourage your child to say other words that end with the same sound.

Harcourt

Name _____

▶ **Think about the story. Write the names of these story characters.**

_____

- - - - - - - - - - - - - - - -

_____

_____

- - - - - - - - - - - - - - - -

_____

▶ **What do the dogs get at the end of the story? Draw a picture and label it.**

_____

- -

_____

SCHOOL-HOME CONNECTION Encourage your child to
tell you about the story *Apple Snacks.* Ask your child
who picks apples and who gets an apple snack.

Open Doors Theme 2
Lesson 9

Harcourt

Name _____

▶ **Read the contractions in the box. Finish each sentence. Write the contraction for the two words that are above the line.**

Here's	Pat's	It's	What's	That's

_____ **Pat is** _____

- - - - - - - - - - - - - - - - - - -

1. _____ here now.

_____ **Here is** _____

- - - - - - - - - - - - - - - - - - -

2. _____ my sack.

_____ **What is** _____

- - - - - - - - - - - - - - - - - - -

3. _____ in it?

_____ **That is** _____

- - - - - - - - - - - - - - - - - - -

4. _____ a surprise.

_____ **It is** _____

- - - - - - - - - - - - - - - - - - -

5. _____ a good surprise.

SCHOOL-HOME CONNECTION Let your child point to two words he or she wrote as a contraction. Help your child think of other pairs of words that can be written together the same way.

Harcourt

Name _____

▶ **Write the words where they belong in the puzzles.**

kick	pick	sack	pack	sick

1.

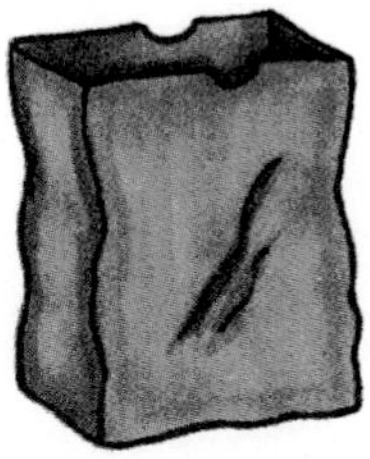

2.

3.

4.

5.

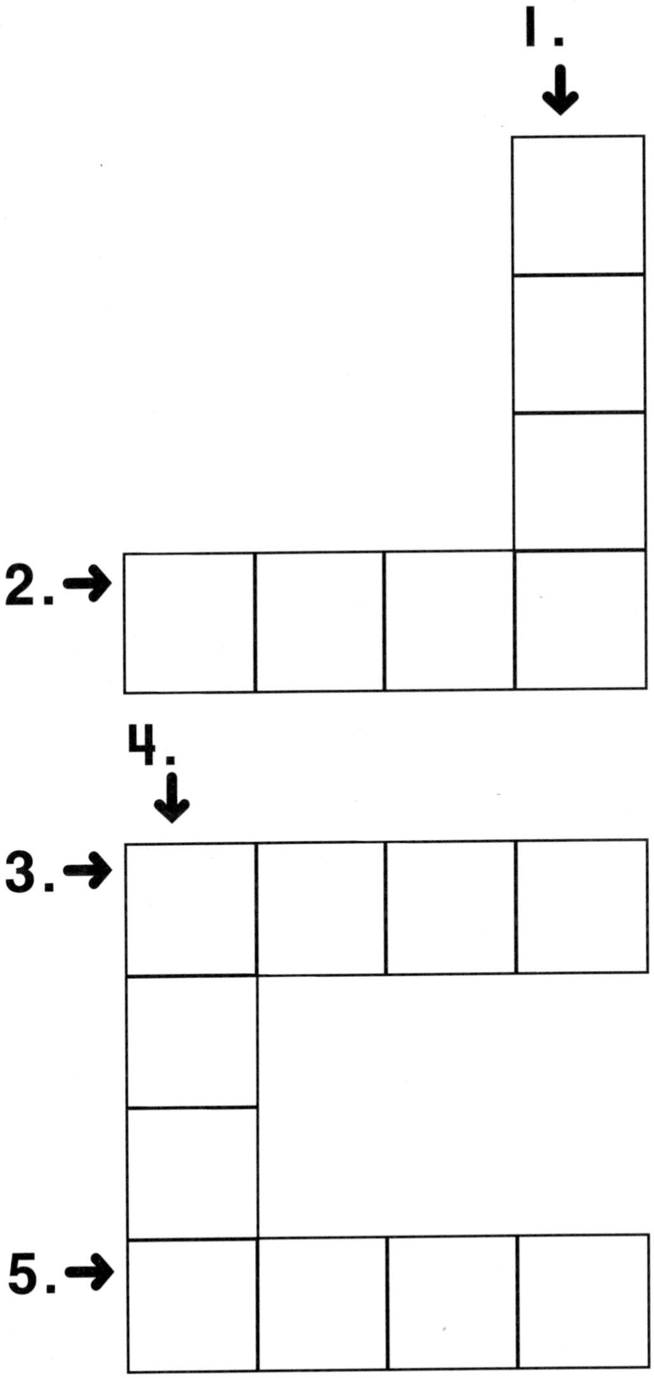

1. ↓

2. →

4. ↓

3. →

5. →

SCHOOL-HOME CONNECTION Let your child read aloud the words he or she wrote in the crossword puzzles. Then ask your child to name people or things that end with the same sounds.

Harcourt

Name _____

▶ **Write the word in the box that names each picture.**

lid	lips	lap	hill

1.

_____

- - - - - - - - - - - - - -

_____

2.

_____

- - - - - - - - - - - - - -

_____

3.

_____

- - - - - - - - - - - - - -

_____

4.

_____

- - - - - - - - - - - - - -

_____

TRY THIS How many words can you make with the following letters? l, a, i, l, t, n, h, p, d

Open Doors Theme 2
Lesson 11

SCHOOL-HOME CONNECTION Ask your child to point out words that begin with *l*. Then encourage your child to make a list of objects with names that begin with the same sound.

Harcourt

Name _____

▶ **Write the naming part of each sentence.**

1. I will sit here.

_____

_____

2. You can sit on that.

_____

_____

3. My dad can sit here.

_____

_____

4. Matt can sit here.

_____

_____

5. His dog can not sit here.

_____

_____

TRY THIS Choose one of the naming parts you wrote. Use it to begin another sentence. Write the new sentence.

 SCHOOL-HOME CONNECTION Encourage your child to tell you what the naming part of a sentence does. Then have your child say several sentences with the naming part *I*.

Open Doors Theme 2
Lesson 11

Harcourt

Name _____

▶ **Write the word that best completes each sentence.**

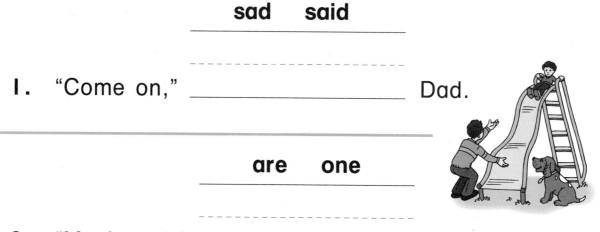

sad   said

_____

1. "Come on," _____ Dad.

are   one

_____

2. "Mack and I _____ here."

dogs   down

_____

3. I slid _____.

growing   cookies

_____

4. "You are _____," said Dad.

said   sat

_____

5. "Look at that," I _____.

Open Doors Theme 2
Lesson 12

SCHOOL-HOME CONNECTION Write the word *said*, and let your child read it to you. Together, read newspaper or magazine captions to find the word *said*.

Harcourt

Name _____

▶ **Write the word from the box that completes the sentence.**

| lid | lap | lick | pal | hill |

1. _____

   Pip can _____.

2. The _____ looks good to Pip.

3. Pip comes down the _____.

4. Pip sits on my _____.

5. Pip is my _____.

Open Doors Theme 2
Lesson 12

Harcourt

Name _____

▶ **Circle the sentences that tell what happens in the story. Then draw a picture to show what happens at the end.**

1. "I am sick," said Sid.

2. "You are not sick," said Sid's pals.

3. "Sit on my lap," said Mom.

4. "You are sick," said Mom.

5. "You are growing," said Mom.

SCHOOL-HOME CONNECTION Have your child tell you about the main character in the story Is Sid Sick? Ask your child what kind of animal he is and why he thought he was sick.

Harcourt

Name _____

▶ **Circle the word that completes each sentence. Then write the word.**

_____
- - - - - - - - - - - -

1. The dogs are in the _____ .

hill
hall
call

_____
- - - - - - - - - - - -

2. Can _____ the dogs pass?

call
all
ill

_____
- - - - - - - - - - - -

3. One dog is too _____ .

lit
tall
all

_____
- - - - - - - - - - - -

4. I _____ that dog Mack.

call
ill
mall

_____
- - - - - - - - - - - -

5. Where are _____ the dogs now?

hall
mall
all

Harcourt

SCHOOL-HOME CONNECTION Ask your child to write the word *all*.
Together, think of words that rhyme with *all*.

Open Doors Theme 2
Lesson 13

65

Name _____

Sid's Rattle

▶ **Write the word that best completes each sentence.**

Will   We

_____

- - - - - - - - - - - - -

1. "_____ see you," said my pals.

we   was

_____

- - - - - - - - - - - - -

2. Where _____ Pam?

it   up

_____

- - - - - - - - - - - - -

3. "Look _____," said Pam.

was   we

_____

- - - - - - - - - - - - -

4. "Here _____ are!" said Jack.

Harcourt

SCHOOL-HOME CONNECTION Talk with your child about opposites.
Ask your child what the opposite of *up* is. Together, think of other
pairs of words with opposite meanings.

Name _____

▶ **Circle the word that completes each sentence. Then write the word.**

_____
- - - - - - - - - - -

1. Look at that _____ .

can
hat
cat

_____

_____
- - - - - - - - - - -

2. He is _____ .

all
tall
call

_____
- - - - - - - - - - -

3. That cat has _____ the hats.

a
at
all

_____
- - - - - - - - - - -

4. One cat is in the _____ .

hat
hall
call

_____
- - - - - - - - - - -

5. I will _____ the cat.

call
cat
can

Harcourt

SCHOOL-HOME CONNECTION Ask your child to point out at least three words that end with the letters -all. Together, think of other words that end with that same sound.

▶ **Think about the story. What did the
story characters say in the beginning,
the middle, and the end of the story? Finish
the sentences.**

Beginning

Sid said,

_____

" _____ "

Middle

Sid's pals said,

_____

" _____ "

End

Sid and his pals said,

_____

" _____ "

SCHOOL-HOME CONNECTION Ask your child
to tell you the story of *Sid's Rattle* in his or her
own words.

Harcourt

Name _____

► **Finish each sentence. Write the contraction for the two words.**

didn't	isn't	don't	hasn't	aren't

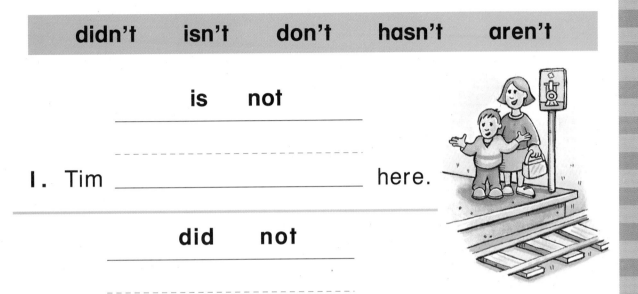

is   not

_____

- -

1. Tim _____ here.

did   not

_____

- -

2. He _____ call me.

are   not

_____

- -

3. His pals _____ here.

do   not

_____

- -

4. I _____ see it.

has   not

_____

- -

5. It _____ come.

SCHOOL-HOME CONNECTION Let your child write the contraction *didn't*. Ask which two words are joined in that contraction.

Open Doors Theme 2
Lesson 15   **69**

Harcourt

Name _____

▶ **Finish each sentence. Put together the word and the word ending. Write the new word.**

look + ed

_____

- - - - - - - - - - - - - - - -

1. Dan _____ for me.

look + ing

_____

- - - - - - - - - - - - - - - -

2. Now I am _____ for him.

call + ed

_____

- - - - - - - - - - - - - - - -

3. He _____ me.

call + ing

_____

- - - - - - - - - - - - - - - -

4. Now I am _____ him.

do + ing

_____

- - - - - - - - - - - - - - - -

5. What is Dan _____?

SCHOOL-HOME CONNECTION Have your child read aloud one of the sentences he or she completed. Ask how the word above the line changed. Encourage your child to make up other sentences using that word.

1

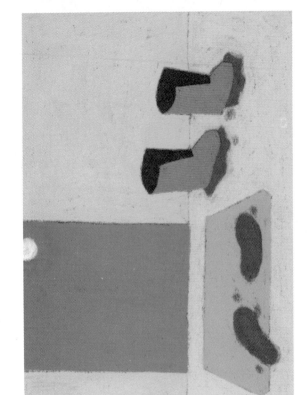

Sam

Fold

Is Sam here?

Harcourt

Fold

Here I am.

8

Is Sam here?

6

Open Doors: Theme 1
Cut-out Fold-up Book

71

4

Is Sam here?

Where *is* Sam?

Harcourt

— Fold —

— Fold —

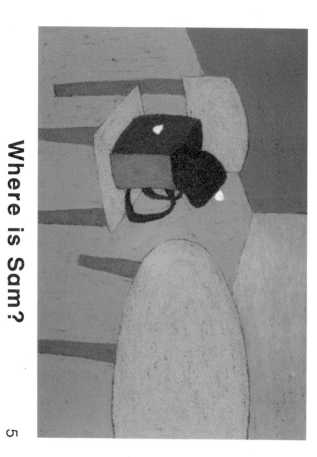

Where is Sam?

Where *is* Sam?

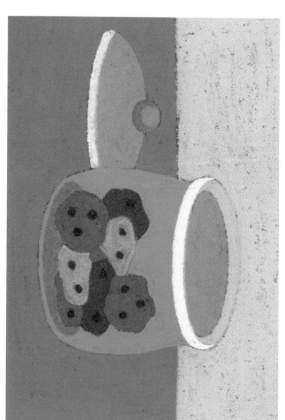

That Cat

1

Fold

Fold

Harcourt

Look at that cat!

3

Here is that cat.

8

Look, cat.

6

Where is that cat?

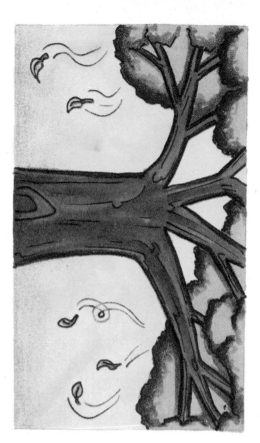

Look!

Come, cat, come!

Come here, cat!

Harcourt

Fold

Fold

Hap and Pam

Harcourt

— Fold —

Where is Pam?

— Fold —

Good! Hap is here.
Pam is here, too.

8

Pam is here.

6

4

Look at the map, Hap.
Look at the map, Pam.

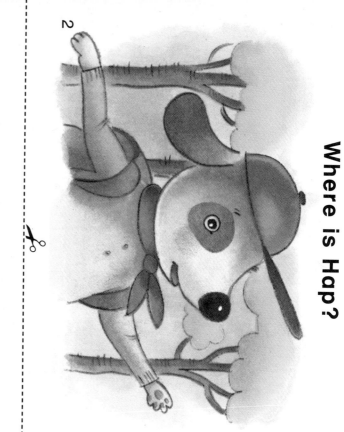

2

Where is Hap?

Harcourt

Fold

Fold

Hap is here.

5

Come here, Hap.
Come here, Pam.

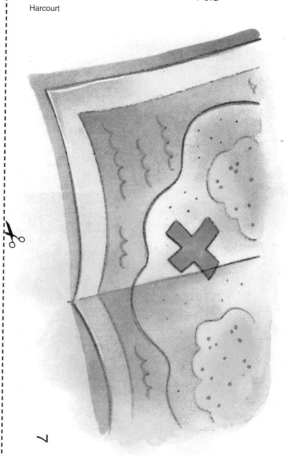

7

Sam and Tim

1

Good dog, Sam!

8

**Look, Sam!
See this?**

3

**Look, Sam!
See this?**

6

Harcourt

— Fold —

— Fold —

4

Come, Sam.
Good dog!

Fold

2

Here come Sam and Tim.

Fold

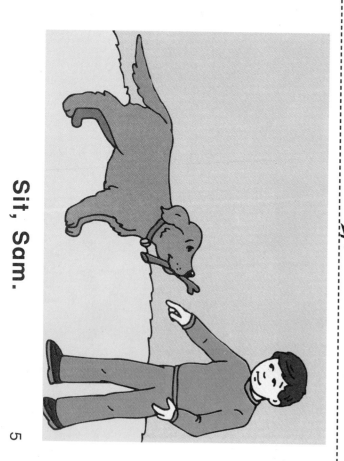

Sit, Sam.

5

What will Sam do?

7

A Sack for You

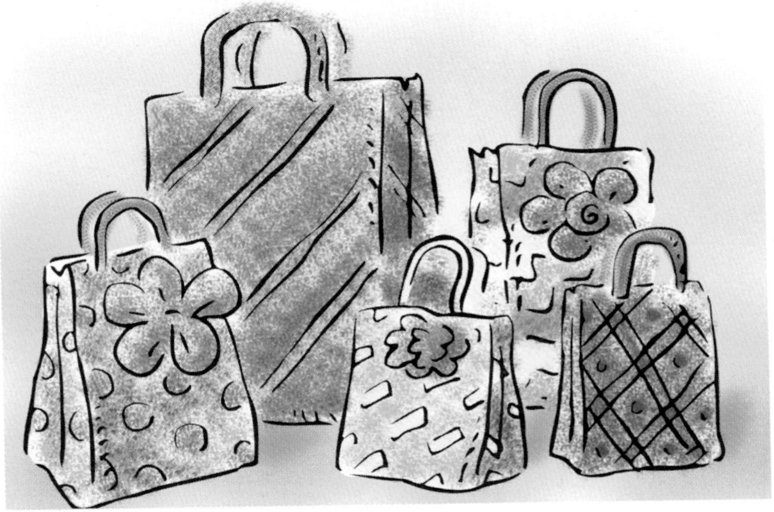

1

Here comes Dan.
Dan has a big sack, too.

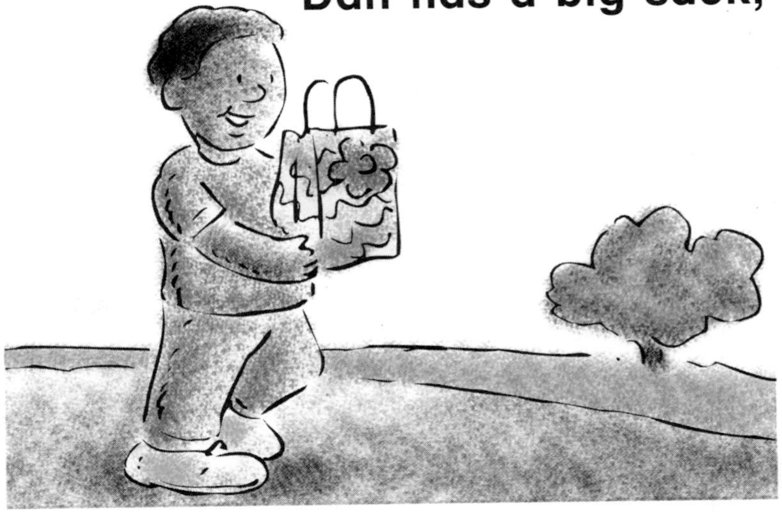

3

Here comes Nan.
Nan has two sacks.

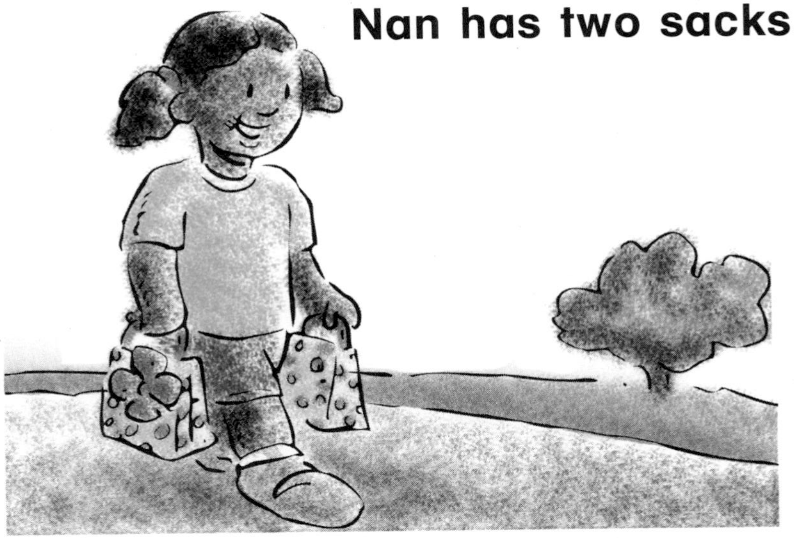

6

What is in it?

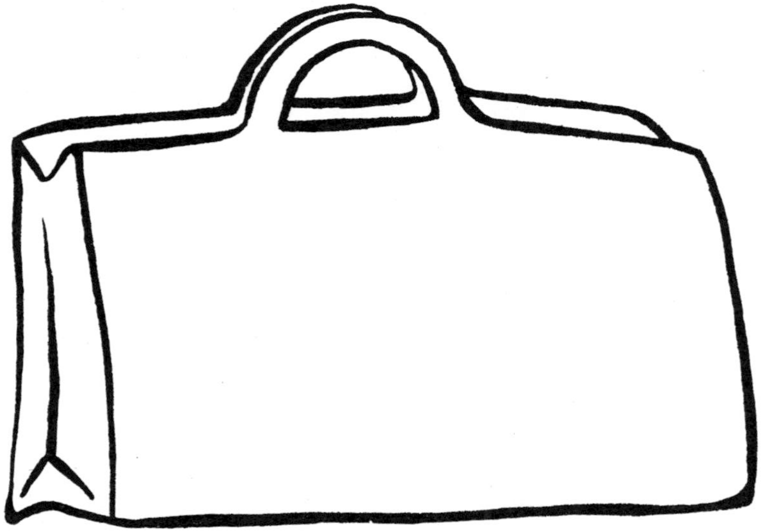

8

Fold

Harcourt

Here comes Pam.
Pam has a sack.

Here comes Kim.
Kim has a big sack.

Harcourt

— Fold —

— Fold —

Pam has a dog.
Pam's dog has a sack.

One sack is for you.
Pick a sack.

Apples

1

An apple was growing here.

3

— Fold —

Harcourt

— Fold —

Isn't that good?

8

And here it is!

6

4

A tall man picked it.

2

Look at this hill.

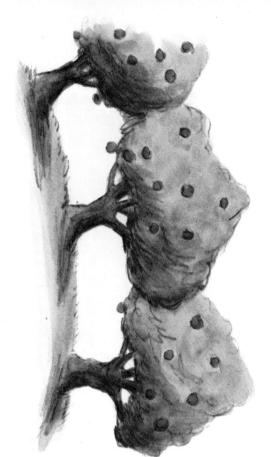

Harcourt

Fold

Fold

He packed it.

5

I see you licking your lips!

7

You're Invited

Name _____

▶ **Look at each picture. Circle the word that completes each sentence. Then write the word.**

sacks   docks   socks

_____

- - - - - - - - - - - - -

1. The _____ are on the mat.

cot   kit   cost

_____

- - - - - - - - - - - - -

2. The dolls are on the _____ .

tip   tot   top

_____

- - - - - - - - - - - - -

3. The caps are on _____ .

pats   pots   pond

_____

- - - - - - - - - - - - -

4. The lids are on the _____ .

Harcourt

SCHOOL-HOME CONNECTION Ask your child to read the words he or she wrote. Look for things in the house whose names have the same short *o* vowel sound.

Name _____

▶ **Join the naming parts of the two sentences. Use the word <u>and</u>. Write the new sentence.**

1. Todd looked. Dog looked.

_____

- - - - - - - - - - - -

_____

- - - - - - - - - - - -

_____

2. Todd slid down. Dog slid down.

_____

- - - - - - - - - - - -

_____

- - - - - - - - - - - -

_____

 TRY THIS Write two sentences about something you and a friend do together. Use the word <u>and</u> to join the naming parts of the two sentences.

SCHOOL-HOME CONNECTION Encourage your child to tell you about sentences that have two naming parts. Together, say some sentences about two family members or friends.

You're Invited
Lesson 1

3

Harcourt

Name _____

▶ **Write the word that best completes
each sentence.**

home   hand   has

_____

- - - - - - - - - - - -

1. Tip is not _____ .

---

now   need   not

_____

- - - - - - - - - - - -

2. We _____ Tip now.

---

help   has   down

_____

- - - - - - - - - - - -

3. We need Tip's _____ !

---

hat   ham   home

_____

- - - - - - - - - - - -

4. Tip! Come _____ !

 TRY THIS Write your own sentence about something you need.
Draw a picture to go with your sentence.

SCHOOL-HOME CONNECTION Write the word
home, and let your child read it aloud. Together,
make up sentences using the word *home*.

Harcourt

Name _____

▶ Say the name of each picture.

Color the picture if the name has the sound /o/.

1.

2.

3.

4.

5.

6.

7.

8.

9.

Harcourt

SCHOOL-HOME CONNECTION Find objects in the house whose names have the short *o* sound as in *hop*. Let your child hop from one short *o* object to the next.

Name _____

▶ **Think about the story. Draw what
happened in the beginning, the middle, and the end.**

Beginning

Middle

Ending

You're Invited
Lesson 2

SCHOOL-HOME CONNECTION Let your
child tell you about the beginning, the
middle, and the end of the story.

Harcourt

▶ **Say the name of the picture. Write <u>th</u> if its name begins or ends with <u>th</u>.**

_____

1. _____

_____

2. _____

_____

3. _____

_____

4. _____

_____

5. _____

_____

6. _____

_____

7. _____

_____

8. _____

_____

9. _____

Harcourt

SCHOOL-HOME CONNECTION Sing together "Where Is Thumbkin?" Encourage your child to add motions by wiggling his or her thumbs as if they are talking to each other.

▶ **Look at each picture. Write the word in the box that best completes each sentence.**

go	our	there	to	walk

1. Can you come _____ my home?

2. I will _____ on my bike.

3. We will _____ .

4. We see _____ mom.

5. Are we _____ now?

SCHOOL-HOME CONNECTION Write the words *go* and *to*, and let your child read them aloud. Ask how the two words are alike and how they are different. Then let your child use the words in a sentence.

Harcourt

Name _____

► **Look at each picture. Write the word in the box that completes each sentence.**

this	thin	path	moth	math

1. The cat hops on the _____.

2. Tom is good at _____.

3. Samson looks too _____.

4.  Can you see the _____?

5. _____ hat looks good on me.

SCHOOL-HOME CONNECTION Say the following words and ask your child to say a rhyming word that begins with the sound *th*: tank (thank), *hum* (thumb), *horn* (thorn), and *tick* (thick).

You're Invited
Lesson 4   9

Harcourt

Name _____

▶ **Think about the story. Circle the words that tell what happened in the story.**

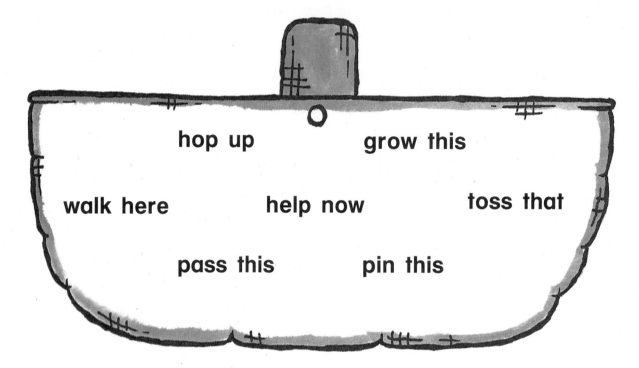

hop up   grow this

walk here   help now   toss that

pass this   pin this

▶ **Draw what happened at the end of the story.**

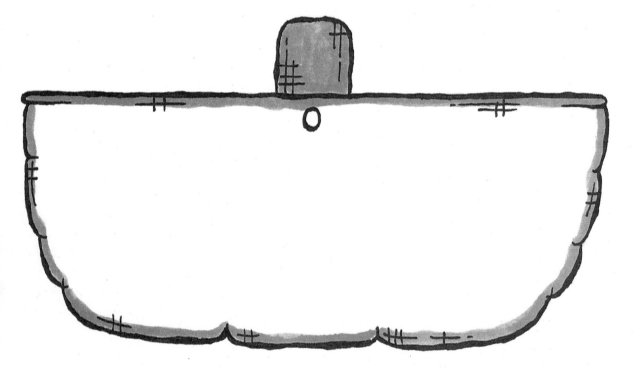

SCHOOL-HOME CONNECTION Ask your child to tell you about the story *The Picnic*. Who packed the picnic? Who else came to the picnic?

Harcourt

Name _____

▶ **Name each picture. Listen to the beginning sounds. Write the two letters that stand for the beginning sounds.**

sk	sl	sn	sp	st

_____

- - - - - - - -

1. _____

_____

- - - - - - - -

2. _____

_____

- - - - - - - -

3. _____

_____

- - - - - - - -

4. _____

_____

- - - - - - - -

5. _____

_____

- - - - - - - -

6. _____

_____

- - - - - - - -

7. _____

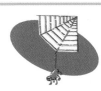

_____

- - - - - - - -

8. _____

_____

- - - - - - - -

9. _____

Harcourt

You're Invited
Lesson 5   **11**

Name _____

▶ **Say the name of the picture. Write g if the name begins with g.**

1. _____

2. _____ g _____

3. _____

4. _____

5. _____

6. _____

7. _____

8. _____

9. _____

SCHOOL-HOME CONNECTION Finish this sentence to plan a silly garden: In my garden, I will grow.... Grow anything whose name begins with the sound of g.

Harcourt

Name _____

▶ **Write the telling part of each sentence.**

1. Zack slid.

_____

- - - - - - - - - - - - - - - - - - -

_____

2. Zack looks.

_____

- - - - - - - - - - - - - - - - - - -

_____

3. He sees.

_____

- - - - - - - - - - - - - - - - - - -

_____

4. He calls.

_____

- - - - - - - - - - - - - - - - - - -

_____

5. I missed you, Mom.

_____

- - - - - - - - - - - - - - - - - - -

_____

Harcourt

SCHOOL-HOME CONNECTION Encourage your child to say several sentences telling what he or she likes to do at home. Together, talk about the telling parts of your child's sentences.

You're Invited
Lesson 6   **13**

Name _____

▶ **Write the word that best completes each sentence.**

for friends fist
_____

- -

1. What can _____ do?

On One Oh
_____

- -

2. _____, friends can hop and skip.

so see sat
_____

- -

3. Friends can sit _____ still, too.

It Is I'm
_____

- -

4. _____ your friend.

fills fins friends
_____

- -

5. We can be good _____.

SCHOOL-HOME CONNECTION Write the word *friends*, and let your child read it to you. Together, talk about what your child enjoys doing with friends.

Harcourt

Name _____

▶ **Read the story. Circle the words that begin with <u>G</u> or <u>g</u>. Underline the words that have the /o/ sound.**

Lost Dog

One day my dog Gil got lost. "Here, Gil!" I called. Gil did not come. Gil was not in the hall. "Are you up, Gil?" I called. "There you are!" Gil had a good nap. "Oh, Gil!" I said. "Let's go."

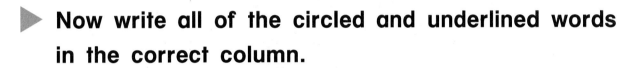

▶ **Now write all of the circled and underlined words in the correct column.**

g	o
1. _____	_____
2. _____	_____
3. _____	_____
4. _____	_____

SCHOOL-HOME CONNECTION Hide a stuffed toy. As your child looks for it, give clues by saying *Good* when he or she gets close and *Not good* when he or she gets farther away. Take turns hiding and finding the toy.

Harcourt

Name _____

▶ **Look at each picture clue in the story chart below. Draw or write where Gil went in the story.**

I.	(faucet dripping)	_____ _____ _____
2.	2/3	_____ _____ _____
3.	(logs)	_____ _____ _____
4.	(ants by anthill)	_____ _____ _____

 TRY THIS Think of a story about someone who is lost. Draw a picture and label it.

SCHOOL-HOME CONNECTION Ask your child to tell you about the ant in the story and how he gets home. Discuss what your child should do if he or she gets lost.

Harcourt

Name _____

► **Look at each picture. Circle the word**
that completes each sentence. Then write the word.

Mom   Todd   Dad

_____

1. This is _____.

---

moss   mitt   toss

_____

2. He has my _____.

Todd   Ann   Dad

_____

3. I am _____.

---

miss   add   mitt

_____

4. I _____ it.

---

pan   pass   mitt

_____

5. Will he _____ it to me?

TRY THIS Draw a picture of something or someone you miss.
Write a sentence to go with your picture.

SCHOOL-HOME CONNECTION Read aloud the words your
child added to the sentences on this page. Ask your child to
clap twice after each word to remember the double consonant.

You're Invited
Lesson 8   **17**

Harcourt

Name _____

▶ **Write the word that best completes each sentence.**

she   saw   so

_____

- - - - - - - - - - - -

1. I _____ my friends.

They   That   This

_____

- - - - - - - - - - - -

2. _____ had bikes.

dip   day   dig

_____

- - - - - - - - - - - -

3. "We will be on our bikes all _____."

they   this   that

_____

- - - - - - - - - - - -

4. "You can come, too," _____ said.

down   do   day

_____

- - - - - - - - - - - -

5. What a great _____ we had!

SCHOOL-HOME CONNECTION Write the word *day*, and let your child read it aloud. Together, review the names of the days of the week.

Harcourt

Name _____

▶ **Look at each picture. Write the word that best completes the sentence.**

mitt	toss	Ann	add	pass

_____

1. I am _____ .

_____

2. This is my _____ .

_____

3. I can _____ the ball.

_____

4. I will _____ first base.

_____

5. I can _____ up the hits!

TRY THIS What can you pass to someone else? Draw a picture of it. Write a sentence to go with your picture.

SCHOOL-HOME CONNECTION Have your child read aloud one of the sentences he or she finished on this page. Ask your child to point out the double letters in the word he or she added.

Harcourt

Name _____

▶ In the story, Gil is happy at the beginning. In the middle, he is sad. Then at the end, he is very happy. Write below to tell why.

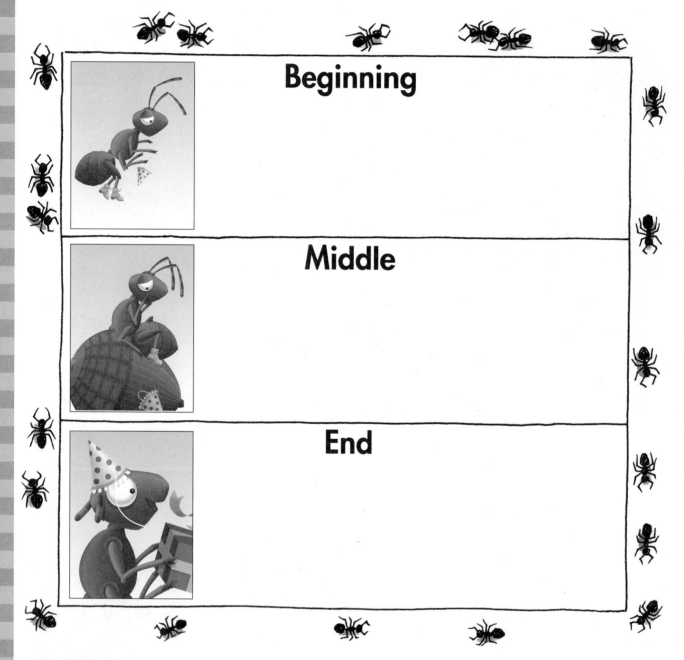

Beginning

Middle

End

TRY THIS What do you think will happen next to Gil and his friends? Draw a picture to show your idea.

SCHOOL-HOME CONNECTION Think of another story you and your child know that has a happy ending. Tell it to one another.

Harcourt

Name _____

▶ **Use the words from the box to complete the rhyme.**

| hang   sang   song   long |

_____

I _____ for my dad.

It was a good _____.

Now I'll _____ up my socks.

And I'll say, "So _____."

TRY THIS Draw a picture of yourself helping out at home. Sing your favorite song softly as you draw.

SCHOOL-HOME CONNECTION Ask your child to help you with a household chore. Sing a song together while you work.

You're Invited
Lesson 10   21

Name _____

▶ **Write the word that best completes each sentence.**

hops   hopped   hopping
_____

- - - - - - - - - - - - - - -

1. The cats _____ down the path.

sits   sat   sitting
_____

- - - - - - - - - - - - - - -

2. A dog was _____ on a log.

stops   stopped   stopping
_____

- - - - - - - - - - - - - - -

3. The cats saw the dog and _____.

tip   tipped   tipping
_____

- - - - - - - - - - - - - - -

4. The dog _____ his hat to the cats.

hop   hopped   hopping
_____

- - - - - - - - - - - - - - -

5. They are all _____ down the path.

SCHOOL-HOME CONNECTION Work together to make a list of the words with *-ed* and *-ing* that you used. Circle any words where you doubled the final consonant.

Harcourt

Name _____

▶ Say the name of the picture. Write **r** if the name begins with **r**.

1. ____r____

2. _____

3. _____

4. _____

5. _____

6. _____

7. _____

8. _____

9. _____

TRY THIS Draw a picture of a rocket. What would you take with you if you flew in a rocket?

SCHOOL-HOME CONNECTION With your child, search through the house for things that are red. Say, "R-r-r-r," each time you find one.

You're Invited
Lesson 11   **23**

Harcourt

Name _____

▶ **Use _and_ to join the telling parts of the two sentences. Write the new sentence.**

I. Pam ran. Pam called the dog.

_____

- - - - - - - - - - - - - - - - - - - -

_____

- - - - - - - - - - - - - - - - - - - -

_____

2. Tip got up. Tip ran.

_____

- - - - - - - - - - - - - - - - - - - -

_____

- - - - - - - - - - - - - - - - - - - -

_____

 TRY THIS Can you do two things at the same time? Write a sentence about what you can do. Draw a picture to go with it.

SCHOOL-HOME CONNECTION With your child, talk about outdoor activities your family enjoys. Use some sentences with telling parts for two things people do.

Name _____

▶ **Write the word from the box that completes the sentence.**

night	played	time	sleep	better

1. Spot and I _____ all day.

2. At _____ Spot and I read a book.

3. Mom said, "It is _____ for bed."

4. "Can Spot _____ on my bed?"

5. I said, "I will sleep

_____ now."

TRY THIS Use the word <u>sleep</u> in a sentence. Draw a picture to go with your sentence.

SCHOOL-HOME CONNECTION Ask your child to read aloud the words in the box. Take turns making up sentences using those words.

You're Invited
Lesson 12 **25**

Harcourt

Name _____

▶ **Look at each picture. Write the word in the box that completes each sentence.**

red	rat	rag	rock	rip

1. Ron is a _____ .

2. He has a _____ hat.

3. He has a big _____ , too.

4. Did he _____ it?

5. Ron goes up the big _____ .

TRY THIS Write your own sentence with the word <u>ran</u>. Draw a picture to go with your sentence.

SCHOOL-HOME CONNECTION Ask your child to say some words that begin with the same sound you hear at the beginning of *rat*. Then have your child practice writing the letter *r*.

Harcourt

Name _____

▶ **Think about the story. Finish the sentences to tell what happened.**

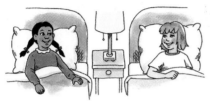

_____

- - - - - - - - - - - - - - - - - -

1. Ronda _____.

_____

- - - - - - - - - - - - - - - - - -

2. It was time to _____.

3. What was that

_____

- - - - - - - - - - - - - - - - - -

_____ ?

4. Ronda saw a tail go

_____

- - - - - - - - - - - - - - - - - -

_____.

_____

- - - - - - - - -

5. It was the _____ !

🎤 **TRY THIS** Think of something else that might be in a scary story.
Draw a picture of it.

Harcourt

Name _____

▶ **Write the word that best completes each sentence.**

list   fast   fin

_____

- - - - - - - - - -

1. Frank can go _____ .

fan   fit   for

_____

- - - - - - - - - -

2. He can go _____ a long time.

at   off   one

_____

- - - - - - - - - -

3. Did Frank get _____ his bike?

fall   hall   fan

_____

- - - - - - - - - -

4. Did he _____?

if   stiff   staff

_____

- - - - - - - - - -

5. Is his leg _____?

28 You're Invited
Lesson 13

SCHOOL-HOME CONNECTION Practice saying this tongue twister with your child: *The first leaf fell off Friday.* Then ask your child to say other words that begin with the sound you hear at the beginning of *fall.*

Harcourt

Name _____

▶ **Read the words in the box. Write the word that best completes each sentence.**

could	her	put	find	who

1. Cass has lost _____ mitt.

2. Can you help her _____ it?

3. Did she _____ it in this big sack?

4. We _____ look in the sack.

5. I see _____ has the mitt!

TRY THIS Sort the vocabulary words by the number of letters they contain.

SCHOOL-HOME CONNECTION Let your child read aloud the words in the box. Together, try to make up a silly sentence using all five words.

You're Invited
Lesson 14 **29**

Harcourt

▶ **Look at each picture. Write the word in the box that best completes each sentence about the picture.**

| fin | fist | fast | fall | stiff | off |

1. It has a big _____.

2. It can go _____.

3. They will come _____.

4. This is my _____.

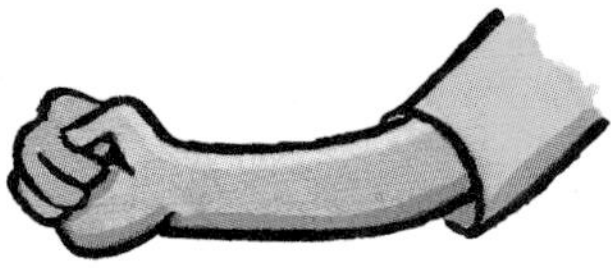

5. It is _____.

6. They will _____.

SCHOOL-HOME CONNECTION Ask your child to read the words in the box. Have your child point out the words that end with the sound you hear at the end of *leaf*. Together, think of other words that end with the f sound.

Harcourt

▶ **Think about the story. Fill in the chart.**
Draw or write your answers.

1. Pat could not find this. _____ - - - - - - - - - - - - - _____	
2. Mom could not find this. _____ - - - - - - - - - - - - - _____	
3. Dad could not find this. _____ - - - - - - - - - - - - - _____	
4. He hid all the things. _____ - - - - - - - - - - - - - _____	

TRY THIS Draw a picture of another adventure about Rip and Pat.

 SCHOOL-HOME CONNECTION Ask your child to tell the story in his or her own words. Then challenge your child to think of a different ending for the story.

You're Invited
Lesson 14   **31**

Harcourt

▶ **Name each picture. Listen to the beginning sounds. Write the two letters that stand for the beginning sound.**

tr	cr	pr	dr	gr	fr

1. _____

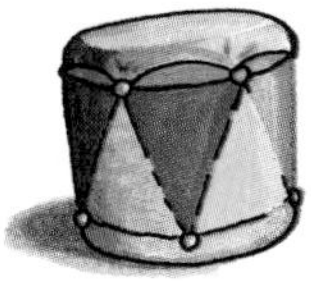

2. _____

3. _____

4. _____

5. _____

6. _____

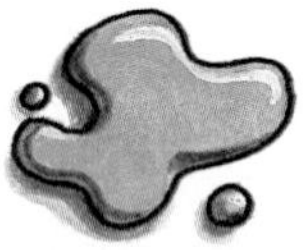

7. _____

8. _____

9. _____

SCHOOL-HOME CONNECTION Ask your child to tell you about the pictures on this page. Together, try to think of other blends that begin with the same sounds you hear at the beginning of the word *train*.

Harcourt

Name _____

▶ **Write the words where they belong in the puzzles.**

bag   crab   bat   ball   crib   cab   bill

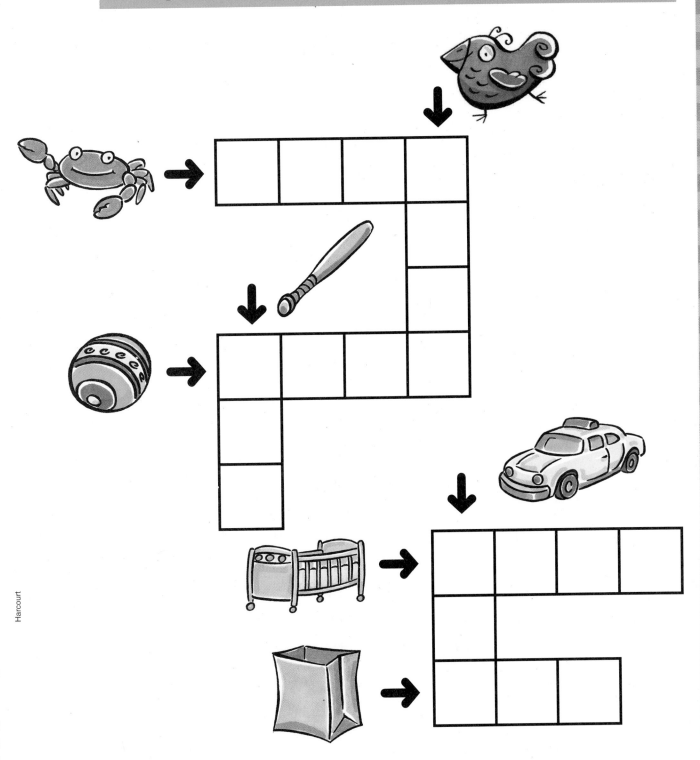

SCHOOL-HOME CONNECTION Ask your child to name some of the pictures. Then have your child practice writing the letter *b*.

You're Invited
Lesson 16   33

Harcourt

▶ **Complete each sentence. Write
either a naming part or a telling part.**

_____

1. Rabbits _____ .

2. _____ can hop.

3. My friends _____ .

4. _____ played.

5. _____ is happy.

 TRY THIS What else can you do? Write a complete sentence
telling about it. If you want, draw a picture to go
with your sentence.

SCHOOL-HOME CONNECTION Ask your child to say a complete
sentence, telling what he or she did today. Encourage your child
to write the sentence.

Harcourt

Name _____

▶ **Write the word that best completes each sentence.**

eyes   again   no

_____

- - - - - - - - - - - - - -

1. I saw two big _____.

no   eyes   again

_____

- - - - - - - - - - - - - -

2. I looked _____.

why   first   again

_____

- - - - - - - - - - - - - -

3. I saw what I saw the _____ time.

Eyes   No   You

_____

- - - - - - - - - - - - - -

4. _____, I did not see that it was you.

Why   Eyes   First

_____

- - - - - - - - - - - - - -

5. _____ did you surprise me like that?

SCHOOL-HOME CONNECTION Read the word *eyes* together.
Have your child draw your portrait and label your eyes.

You're Invited
Lesson 17   35

Harcourt

Phonics

Consonants:
/b/b, /r/r
Short Vowel: /o/o

▶ **Look at each picture. Circle the word that completes the sentence. Then write the word.**

crab   crib   cab

_____

1.

Bill was in the _____.

bid   tab   bib

_____

2.

He had a big _____.

sob   cob   bat

_____

3.

Why did Bill _____?

rib   bad   rob

_____

4.

Did the cat _____ him?

brick   bath   back

_____

5.

Bill was happy in the _____.

SCHOOL-HOME CONNECTION Ask your child to read one of the sentences he or she completed on this page. Together, think of names for people or pets that begin with the letter *B*.

Harcourt

Name _____

▶ **Think about the story. Draw or write
what happened to each animal's eyes in the story.**

Before	After

TRY THIS In many stories, the main character changes. Think
of a story you like. Write about one of the characters
in the story.

SCHOOL-HOME CONNECTION With your child, have
fun making up a legend about why owls say "WHO!"

You're Invited
Lesson 17   37

Harcourt

Name _____

▶ **Write the word in the box that names each picture.**

| fort | corn | thorn | horn | fork | torn |

1.

_____

- - - - - - - - - - - - - - -

_____

2.

_____

- - - - - - - - - - - - - - -

_____

3.

_____

- - - - - - - - - - - - - - -

_____

4.

_____

- - - - - - - - - - - - - - -

_____

5.

_____

- - - - - - - - - - - - - - -

_____

6.

_____

- - - - - - - - - - - - - - -

_____

TRY THIS Write your own sentence with the word <u>or</u>. Draw a picture to go with your sentence.

38 You're Invited
Lesson 18

SCHOOL-HOME CONNECTION Ask your child to write the word *or*. Then have your child say several other words that include the *or* sound.

Harcourt

Name _____

▶ **Read the words in the box. Write the word that best completes each sentence.**

out	eat	of	gone	were

1. What can we _____?

2. The good things are _____!

3. There _____ some good snacks.

4. We have one can _____ food.

FOOD

5. We can go _____ for a good snack.

TRY THIS Draw a picture of something you like to eat. Write a sentence to go with your picture.

SCHOOL-HOME CONNECTION With your child, talk about foods your family likes to eat. Ask your child to help you prepare a snack or a meal.

Harcourt

Name _____

▶ **Finish the story. Write the word in the box that completes each sentence.**

Bob	for	corn	born

Mort's Pig

"I like your pig," said Ann.

_____

"He was _____ on Monday," Mort said.

_____

"I will call him _____."

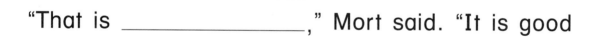

Ann asked, "What is he eating?"

_____

"That is _____," Mort said. "It is good

_____

_____ pigs."

SCHOOL-HOME CONNECTION Ask your chnild to write the word *born*. Discuss the date on which he or she was born.

Harcourt

Name _____

▶ **Look at the chart and answer the
questions. Use what you learned in the story.**

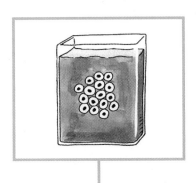

1. Where do frogs come from?

2. What are they called at first?

3. How do frogs change?

4. What do big frogs do? What do
they eat?

Harcourt

SCHOOL-HOME CONNECTION Ask your child what he or
she learned about frogs in this story. What else would he
or she like to know? Look it up at the library.

You're Invited
Lesson 19   **41**

▶ **Look at the pictures. Write the word in the box that best completes each sentence.**

masks	stork	stacks	sticks	spots

I. Where is the _____?

2. I see two _____.

3. The dog has three _____.

4. I see two _____ of blocks.

5. I see lots of _____.

TRY THIS Write a sentence about your favorite sport. Draw a picture to go with your sentence.

SCHOOL-HOME CONNECTION Ask your child to write the word *list*. You may want to say the word slowly to help your child write the letter that stands for each sound. Then have your child suggest other words that end with the *-st* sounds.

Harcourt

Name _____

▶ **Look at each picture. Circle the word that completes the sentence. Then write the word.**

_____

- - - - - - - - - - - - - - - - -

drill
trot
trick

 1. My horse will _____.

_____

- - - - - - - - - - - - - - - - -

grass
grin
drip

 2. This _____ is tall.

_____

- - - - - - - - - - - - - - - - -

crank
from
cross

3. Can we _____ here?

_____

- - - - - - - - - - - - - - - - -

trim
drink
drip

4. The horses _____.

 TRY THIS Where would you like to go? Write your own sentence with the word <u>trip</u>. Draw a picture to go with your sentence.

SCHOOL-HOME CONNECTION Have your child read aloud one of the words he or she wrote on this page. Ask your child to say other words that begin with the same pair of letters as that word does.

You're Invited
Lesson 20   **43**

Harcourt

Name _____

▶ **Look at each picture. Use a word in the box to complete each sentence.**

| wag | wings | wick | wink | swim |

1. It has a _____
   _____ .

2. It has a tail to _____ .

3. It can _____ .

4. It has two _____ .

5. It can _____ .

TRY THIS Think of something to write a clue about. When you write your clue, try to use words that describe it.

44 You're Invited
Lesson 21

SCHOOL-HOME CONNECTION Ask your child to read some of the words he or she wrote on this page. Then have your child practice writing the letter *w*.

Harcourt

▶ **Read both words above each line.**
Choose the naming word that best completes
the sentence.

friend   **fish**

1. I play with my _____.

snacks   **socks**

2. We eat _____ first.

bill   **ball**

3. Then we toss the _____.

eyes   **fish**

----

4. We look for big _____.

Harcourt

Name _____

▶ **Write the word that best completes each sentence.**

look   like   lick

_____

- - - - - - - - - - - - - -

1. I _____ these cookies.

want   walk   what

_____

- - - - - - - - - - - - - -

2. Do you _____ one?

big   bat   but

_____

- - - - - - - - - - - - - -

3. These cookies are good, _____ they are small.

see   saw   some

_____

- - - - - - - - - - - - - -

4. I could eat _____ cookies.

lost   just   fast

_____

- - - - - - - - - - - - - -

5. I will eat _____ one cookie.

SCHOOL-HOME CONNECTION Write the word *want* and let your child read it to you. Then talk about things you want to do together.

Harcourt

Name _____

Phonics

Consonants:
/w/w, /g/g
Digraph: /th/th

▶ **Write the words where they belong in the puzzle.**

| wing | gas | swing | think | wig | wag |

1.

2.

3.

4.

5.

6.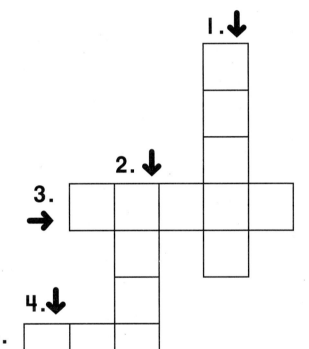

SCHOOL-HOME CONNECTION Encourage your child to share the crossword puzzle he or she completed by reading some of the words aloud. Then ask your child to say other words that begin with the letter *w*.

You're Invited
Lesson 22   47

Harcourt

Name _____

▶ **Think about the story. Fill in the chart below.**

What Wink Wants to Do	Why She Can't

What Wink Does	How She Does It

TRY THIS Think of another way Wink could get a fish. Write or draw it.

You're Invited
Lesson 22

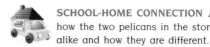 **SCHOOL-HOME CONNECTION** Ask your child to tell you how the two pelicans in the story—Wink and Stan—are alike and how they are different.

Harcourt

Name _____

▶ **Write the word in the box that names each picture.**

dish	ship	flash	shop	fish	shack

1.

_____

- - - - - - - - - - - -

_____

2.

_____

- - - - - - - - - - - -

_____

3.

_____

- - - - - - - - - - - -

_____

4.

_____

- - - - - - - - - - - -

_____

5.

_____

- - - - - - - - - - - -

_____

6.

_____

- - - - - - - - - - - -

_____

TRY THIS Finish this sentence: I wish _____.

Draw a picture to go with your sentence.

SCHOOL-HOME CONNECTION Ask your child to write the word *fish*. Then have your child say several other words that include the /sh/ sound.

You're Invited
Lesson 23 **49**

Harcourt

Name _____

▶ **Write the word that best completes each sentence.**

again   another   ago

_____

- -

1. Here comes _____ friend.

more   my   mom

_____

- -

2. Some _____ friends will come.

The   This   Then

_____

- -

3. _____ we can all go on our bikes.

hand   here   have

_____

- -

4. Do you _____ a bike?

an   another   are

_____

- -

5. No. I will come _____ time.

 **SCHOOL-HOME CONNECTION** With your child, talk about your family's typical daily schedule. Encourage your child to use the word *then*.

Harcourt

Name _____

▶ **Look at each picture. Circle the word
that completes the sentence. Then write the word.**

1. I _____ I were tall.

worn
wish
dash

2. I am not _____.

shop
shock
short

3. I want to _____.

fish
flash
fort

4. I play the _____.

corn
cash
horn

5. I want to play _____.

spots
sports
shots

TRY THIS Write your own sentence with the word <u>dish</u>. Draw a
picture to go with your sentence.

SCHOOL-HOME CONNECTION Ask your child to read aloud
one of the sentences he or she completed. Have your child point
out the two letters that spell the /sh/ sound or the /ôr/ sound.

Harcourt

Name _____

▶ **Look at the picture clues. Write what
happened in the story.**

1. Stan did not like
_____
- - - - - - - - - - - - - - - - - - - -
_____

2. Stan wished he were a
_____
- - - - - - - - - - - - - - - - - - - -
_____

3. Stan did not like
_____
- - - - - - - - - - - - - - - - - - - -
_____

4. Stan wished he were a
_____
- - - - - - - - - - - - - - - - - - - -
_____

5. Stan did not like
_____
- - - - - - - - - - - - - - - - - - - -
_____

6. Stan wished he were a
_____
- - - - - - - - - - - - - - - - - - - -
_____

SCHOOL-HOME CONNECTION Ask your child to tell you
all about Stan's story. Discuss why his wishes were silly.

Harcourt

Name _____

▶ **Finish each sentence. Add es to the word above the line.**

splash

_____

- - - - - - - - - - - - - - - - - - - -

1. The fish _____ .

dish

_____

- - - - - - - - - - - - - - - - - - - -

2. Look at the _____ .

wish

_____

- - - - - - - - - - - - - - - - - - - -

3. Tim _____ for some help.

wash

_____

- - - - - - - - - - - - - - - - - - - -

4. Cass _____ her dog.

TRY THIS Write your own sentence with the word <u>swishes</u>. Draw a picture to go with your sentence.

SCHOOL-HOME CONNECTION Have your child read aloud some of the words he or she wrote on this page. Together, think of other words ending with *sh* that take the ending *-es*.

Harcourt

▶ **Complete each sentence. Write the contraction for the two words above the line.**

I   will
_____

- - - - - - - - - - - - - - - -

1. _____ go to the top.

Who   will
_____

- - - - - - - - - - - - - - - -

2. _____ come with me?

You   will
_____

- - - - - - - - - - - - - - - -

3. _____ like it up here!

He   will
_____

- - - - - - - - - - - - - - - -

4. _____ go up first.

I   will
_____

- - - - - - - - - - - - - - - -

5. _____ see you at the top!

Harcourt

SCHOOL-HOME CONNECTION Ask your child to point out one of the contractions he or she wrote. Then have your child identify the two words that are combined in that contraction.

Name _____

▶ **Write the word in the box that names each picture.**

| net | bell | pen | desk | bed | men | web | sled | ten |

1.

_____

- - - - - - - - - - - -

_____

2.

_____

- - - - - - - - - - - -

_____

3.

_____

- - - - - - - - - - - -

_____

4.

_____

- - - - - - - - - - - -

_____

5.

_____

- - - - - - - - - - - -

_____

6.

_____

- - - - - - - - - - - -

_____

7.

_____

- - - - - - - - - - - -

_____

8.

_____

- - - - - - - - - - - -

_____

9.

_____

- - - - - - - - - - - -

_____

Harcourt

SCHOOL-HOME CONNECTION Use the words on this page to explore short vowel sounds. Substitute the *e* in each word with another vowel (*ten, tan*). Talk about the new words (or nonsense words) that are created.

You're Invited
Lesson 26 **55**

▶ **Look at each picture. Circle the word that completes the sentence. Then write the word.**

want   went   sent

_____

1. Greg _____ to the park.

met   bet   bat

_____

2. He _____ Tess there.

pit   pat   pet

_____

3. Tess had her new _____.

hem   hen   hint

_____

4. It was a _____.

TRY THIS Write your own sentence with the word <u>let</u>. Draw a picture to go with your sentence.

SCHOOL-HOME CONNECTION Ask your child to name some of the pictures on page 55. Have your child point out the *e* in each word in the box on that page.

Harcourt

▶ **Write the words that name a person or a place in each sentence.**

1. Mother is on the hill.

_____   _____

_____   _____

2. Dad walks to the pond.

_____   _____

_____   _____

3. The girl has a doll.

_____

_____

4. My sister has a pet at school.

_____   _____

_____   _____

5. The boys watch the tadpoles.

_____

_____

Harcourt

Name _____

▶ **Look at the pictures. Read the words in the box. Write the word that best completes each sentence.**

every	four	when	would	five

_____

1. He has _____ dogs.

2. She has _____ cats.

3. They are good to _____ pet.

4. The cats play _____ we sleep.

5. What _____ the dogs like?

TRY THIS Draw a picture of five things you like. Write a sentence to go with your picture.

SCHOOL-HOME CONNECTION Write the words *four* and *five*, and let your child read them to you. Then ask your child to point out four things that are alike in some way.

Name _____

Phonics
Short Vowel: /e/e
Consonant: /w/w
Digraph: /sh/sh

▶ **Read each sentence. Add to the pictures.**

1.

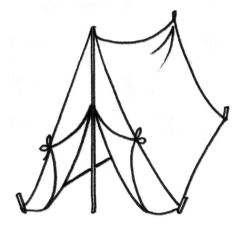

This tent is red.

2.

Now there are six shells.

3.

This web is wet.

4.

I am on the sled.

SCHOOL-HOME CONNECTION Encourage your child to share the pictures he or she has drawn. Ask your child how he or she knew what to draw.

Harcourt

Name _____

▶ **Think about the story. Put a check beside the things that happen in the story. Do not check things that did not happen.**

1. Mom and Pop Nash lost eggs. ☐

2. Mom and Pop Nash saw a fox. ☐

3. They saw a wolf. ☐

4. That morning, there were 11 eggs. ☐

5. They put a net on the wolf. ☐

6. They put a net on Mom Nash. ☐

7. The wolf got some eggs. ☐

8. They got the wolf in a trap. ☐

9. The wolf was eating the eggs. ☐

10. The wolf painted the eggs. ☐

11. They would sell the eggs. ☐

TRY THIS Think of another way to catch the wolf. Draw a picture of it.

SCHOOL-HOME CONNECTION Ask your child to explain the problem in the story Get That Pest! Have him or her explain how the problem was solved.

Harcourt

▶ **Write the word in the box that best completes each sentence.**

Fox	mix	box	Ox	six

1. Help me _____ this snack.

2. _____ will help me.

3. It will fit in this _____.

4. Happy Birthday, _____!

5. My _____ friends can eat with me.

TRY THIS Write your own sentence with the word <u>fix</u>. Draw a picture to go with your sentence.

SCHOOL-HOME CONNECTION Ask your child to spell the word *ox*. Then ask your child to say other words that have the /ks/ sound.

Harcourt

Name _____

▶ **Read the words in the box. Write the word that best completes each sentence.**

very	old	three	jump	how

1. Can you _____ to me?

2. You can do it in _____ jumps.

3. I will come in one _____ long jump.

4. Oh, I see _____ you can do it.

5. That is an _____ trick.

6. _____ did you do it?

TRY THIS One of the vocabulary words can be used to ask a question. Use that word in an asking sentence.

SCHOOL-HOME CONNECTION Let your child read aloud the words in the box. Together, try to make up one sentence that uses all five words.

Harcourt

Name _____

Phonics

Consonants:
/f/f, ff; /ks/x
Short Vowels:
/o/o, /e/e

▶ **Circle the sentence that tells about the picture.**

1.

The fox is on the ox.

The box is on the fox.

The ox is on the box.

2.

One man brings a bag.

Two men bring a box.

Two men bring an ox.

3.

The fox gets in the box.

The ox gets off the box.

The fox gets off the ox.

4.

The fox sits on the box.

The fox steps on the ox.

The ox steps on the box.

5.

The fox fixes the box.

The men fix the box.

The men sit on the ox.

Harcourt

SCHOOL-HOME CONNECTION Have your child describe one of the pictures on this page and read aloud the sentence he or she circled. Ask your child what is wrong with the other sentences.

You're Invited
Lesson 29

Name _____

▶ **Think about the story. Look at each picture. Write a word that tells how the foxes felt in the story.**

What the Foxes Did	How the Foxes Felt
1. 	_____
2. 	_____
3. 	_____
4.  	_____

TRY THIS Think of one more thing these silly foxes might do. Draw a picture of it.

SCHOOL-HOME CONNECTION Talk with your child about the story *Six Silly Foxes*. Ask your child what makes the foxes so silly.

Harcourt

Name _____

▶ **Write the word from the box that best completes each sentence.**

| fast | last | step | snack | spill |

_____

1. You have to _____ up.

_____

2. He goes _____.

_____

3. Let's get a _____.

_____

4. Don't _____ your drink.

_____

5. This is the _____ stop.

Harcourt

SCHOOL-HOME CONNECTION Encourage your child to read aloud some of the sentences he or she finished on this page. Together, think of other words that begin or end with blends with *s*.

You're Invited
Lesson 30   65

Name _____

▶ **Write the two letters in the box that stand for the beginning sounds of each picture name.**

fr	tr	dr	gr	br	cr

1.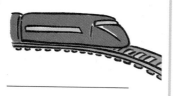

_____

- - - - - - -

_____

2.

_____

- - - - - - -

_____

3.

_____

- - - - - - -

_____

4.

_____

- - - - - - -

_____

5.

_____

- - - - - - -

_____

6.

_____

- - - - - - -

_____

7.

_____

- - - - - - -

_____

8.

_____

- - - - - - -

_____

9.

_____

- - - - - - -

_____

SCHOOL-HOME CONNECTION Ask your child to look at the letter pairs in the box. Encourage your child to find other things in your house that begin with the sounds of the letter combinations *fr, tr, dr, gr, br,* and *cr.*

Harcourt

What Can You Do?

1

Pam has a doll.

3

Fold

Harcourt

Fold

What can you do?

8

This is what Stan has.
Go to it, Stan.

9

4

This is what Nan has.
There is a lot!

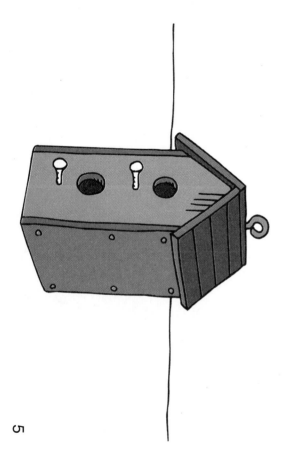

— Fold —

2

This is what Pam has.
Do you need help, Pam?

Harcourt

— Fold —

Now she has a small home.

5

It looks good, Stan.

7

Do You See It?

3

I saw it on Monday.
I think I lost it in here.

— Fold —

Harcourt

— Fold —

What a good day!
We are happy at last.

8

Where is my cat?
That cat is my friend.

6

Where is my snack?
I think the dog has it.

Where is my pig?
It's so soft and pink.

Harcourt

Fold

Fold

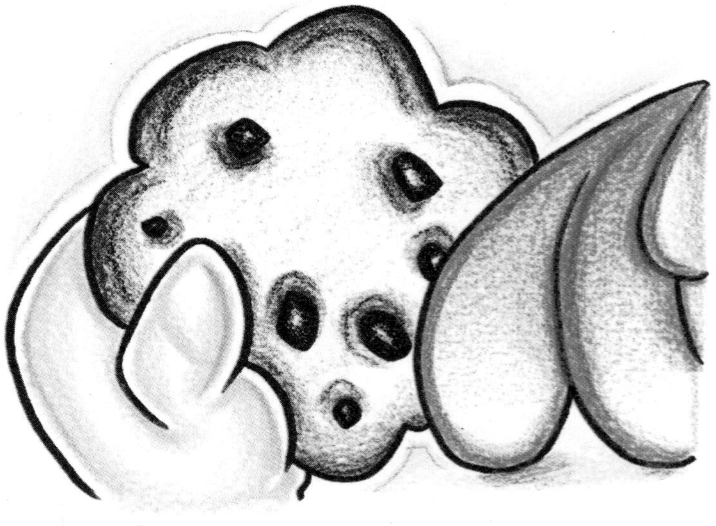

Stop, dog!
I'm big and quick.

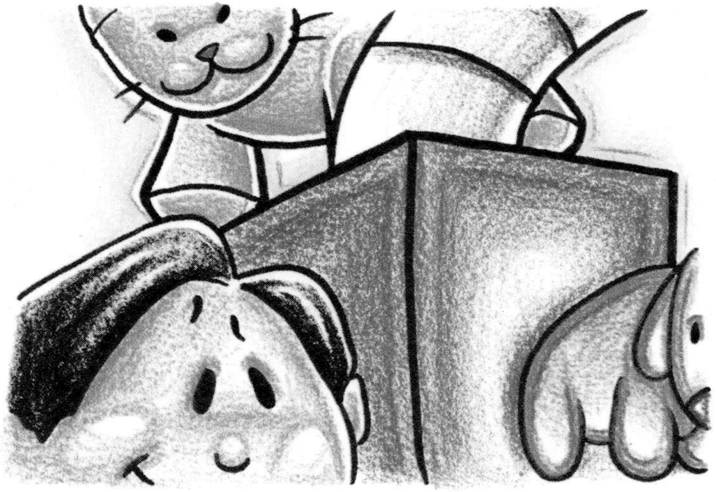

I saw it go up there. Do you
think the cat sees me?

Friends

1

Frank played in the grass.
Red played in the grass, too.

3

Harcourt

Fold

Fold

Red grinned. "Are we still
friends?" Frank grinned, too.

8

Frank slipped.
Red slipped, too.

6

4

Frank sat on a rock.
Red sat on a rock, too.

"Let's be friends," said Red.
"We could have a good time."

Fold

Harcourt

Fold

Frank ran off.
Red ran off, too.

5

"You tricked me!" said Frank.
"I did not," said Red.

7

Be a Sport

1

— Fold —

— Fold —

Where is the mitt?
Do you need all that?

3

I can't do it all.

8

Why don't you help
so we can play ball?

6

4

First sort this string.
Can't your eyes see?

2

Did you bring the ball?
Did you bring the bat?

We have to go out.
Be a good friend to me.

5

Be a good sport, my friend.

7

Just One More

1

—— Fold ——

Harcourt

"Mom, I want another cookie."

3

—— Fold ——

"I want a kiss!"

8

"We have just one more cookie," said Mom.

"Then no more cookies."

6

2

"This cookie is good.
I want just one more."

"I like this cookie, but I wish
for just one more thing, Mom."

7

— Fold —

4

"Here is a cookie. Put it
in your dish," said Mom.

"This cookie is good,
but I want another."

5

— Fold —

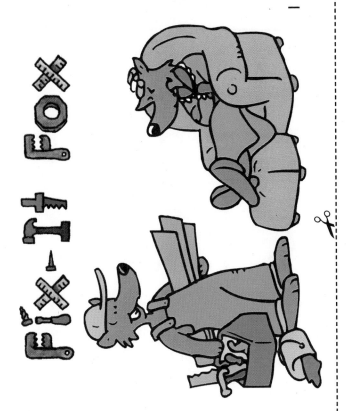

Fix-It Fox

1

"Yes, my pet," said Fox.

3

Harcourt

"My sweet Peg, now who will fix me?"

8

"Fox!" shouted Peg. "I am getting very wet! How long will it be to fix the old well?"

6

"Fox!" shouted Peg. "This is a very big mess. When will you finish the shed?"

"Fox!" shouted Peg. "I would like to rest. Will you fix the three legs on the bed?"

Fold

Harcourt

Fold

"I'll be quick," said Fox.

"In no time," said Fox.

Bright
Ideas

Name _____

▶ **Circle the word that best completes the sentence. Write the word.**

stick

thick

chick

1. The _____ rips

his yellow hat.

Fat

Fetch

Fish

2. "_____ my pins,"

says Mom Hen.

patch

pan

pat

3. Mom Hen makes a small

_____ .

stiff

stitch

sting

4. She will _____ it on.

skill

hill

chill

5. Now Chick will not get a

_____ .

SCHOOL-HOME CONNECTION Chat with your child about how to dress in chilly weather.

Harcourt

Name _____

▶ **Write the words in the barn that name animals. Write the words in the house that name things.**

worm lamp bed pig apple cat horse bike

1. _____

2. _____

3. _____

4. _____

5. _____

6. _____

7. _____

8. _____

TRY THIS Draw a picture of an animal you like. Label the picture.

SCHOOL-HOME CONNECTION Look through a photo album or magazine with your child. Think of as many different words as you can to name each thing or animal.

Harcourt

► **Write the word that best completes each sentence.**

red   ride   rid

_____

- - - - - - - - - - - - - -

1. We had a good _____.

rid   run   ran

_____

- - - - - - - - - - - - - -

2. Will you _____ out back?

of   one   over

_____

- - - - - - - - - - - - - -

3. We jumped _____ a log.

Yes   Yell   You

_____

- - - - - - - - - - - - - -

4. _____, we want to ride.

cried   cord   catch

_____

- - - - - - - - - - - - - -

5. We all _____,

"Can we ride again?"

SCHOOL-HOME CONNECTION Write each vocabulary word on a separate slip of paper, and put the papers face down on a table. Take turns selecting a slip of paper and reading the word on it. Continue until your child has read each word several times.

Harcourt

Name _____

▶ **Circle the sentence that tells about each picture.**

1. Chip likes to chop the ball.
   Chip likes to pitch the ball.
   Chip likes to sketch the ball.

2. Rich can not catch the ball.
   Rich can catch the ball.
   Rich chats with Chip.

3. The friends play hopscotch.
   The friends hop in the ditch.
   The friends sit on a bench.

4. Wag can hatch a chick.
   Wag can get on the branch.
   Wag can fetch the stick.

5. Chet is the champ.
   Chet chomps on an apple.
   Chet checks the chimp.

Harcourt

SCHOOL-HOME CONNECTION Watch part of a sports game together. Talk about the rules. Ask your child to draw a picture of a sports champion.

Name _____

▶ **Write the phrases in the order in which
they happened.**

past the duck pond	past the pig pen	over a ditch
out of the nest	past the horse	

Where did the egg roll?

1. _____

2. _____

3. _____

4. _____

5. _____

TRY THIS Draw a picture to show how the story ended.

Bright Ideas
Lesson 2

6

SCHOOL-HOME CONNECTION Ask your child to use the phrases
and pictures to tell you the story of *The Chick That Wouldn't Hatch*.

Harcourt

Name _____

▶ **Write the word from the box that names each picture.**

| candle | rattle | pickle | apple | bottle | kettle |

1.

_____

- - - - - - - - - - - - - -

_____

2.

_____

- - - - - - - - - - - - - -

_____

3.

_____

- - - - - - - - - - - - - -

_____

4.

_____

- - - - - - - - - - - - - -

_____

5.

_____

- - - - - - - - - - - - - -

_____

6.

_____

- - - - - - - - - - - - - -

_____

Harcourt

SCHOOL-HOME CONNECTION Say these words that end in *le*: *wiggle, giggle, cackle, paddle, tickle.* Let your child act out the words.

Name _____

▶ **Write the word in the box that best completes each sentence.**

fly	other	does	know	answer

_____

1. Sid sat on the _____ side of Sam.

_____

2. "Do you _____ what you

want to do?" asks Sid.

_____

3. "What is your _____?"

_____

4. What _____ Sam want to do?

_____

5. Does he want to _____?

TRY THIS What do you think Sam's answer is? Write two
or three sentences. Use at least two words from
the box.

Bright Ideas
Lesson 4

 SCHOOL-HOME CONNECTION Write the word *answer*, and
have your child read it aloud. Together, write new sentences
using that word.

Harcourt

Name _____

▶ **Read the riddles. Choose the best answer and write it on the line.**

1. Ducks do it when they walk.

Is it **waddle**, **rattle**, or **wall**?

_____

- - - - - - - - - - - - - - - -

_____

2. You do it if you are happy.

Is it **giggle**, **good**, or **grill**?

_____

- - - - - - - - - - - - - - - -

_____

3. It is not big.

Is it **let**, **list**, or **little**?

_____

- - - - - - - - - - - - - - - -

_____

4. It makes a good snack.

Is it **again**, **apple**, or **all**?

_____

- - - - - - - - - - - - - - - -

_____

5. You can make something to eat in it.

Is it **cackle**, **kettle**, or **kid**?

_____

- - - - - - - - - - - - - - - -

_____

6. You can put this in a sandwich.

Is it **play**, **pickle**, or **pimple**?

_____

- - - - - - - - - - - - - - - -

_____

Harcourt

SCHOOL-HOME CONNECTION Ask your child to read each riddle to family members and challenge them to guess the answers.

▶ **Look at the picture. Write a riddle for each picture. You may use your own words.**

1. _____

2. _____

▶ **Now make up a riddle to make Dill Pickle giggle.**

_____

SCHOOL-HOME CONNECTION Have a stand-up comedy night at home. Ask family members to take turns telling jokes, stories, and riddles.

Harcourt

Name _____

► **Write <u>cl</u>, <u>fl</u>, or <u>pl</u> to complete each word.**

_____

- - - - - - - - - - -

1. Milt can do a _____ip.

_____

- - - - - - - - - - -

2. Milt has a _____ant.

_____

- - - - - - - - - - -

3. A _____ag pops out.

_____

- - - - - - - - - - -

4. It's a _____ock.

_____

- - - - - - - - - - -

5. We giggle and _____ap.

TRY THIS Draw a clown doing a funny trick. Write a title for your picture.

SCHOOL-HOME CONNECTION Ask your child to read the sentences to you. Work together to think of more words that begin with the same sounds as *plant*, *flag*, and *clock*.

Bright Ideas
Lesson 5   **11**

Harcourt

Name _____

▶ **Name each picture. Write _ar_ if the name has _ar_ in it.**

1. c_____

2. c_____d

3. c_____n

4. sc_____f

5. h_____se

6. h_____p

7. h_____n

8. st_____

9. b_____n

TRY THIS Make a greeting card. Give it to a friend or family member.

Bright Ideas
Lesson 6
12

SCHOOL-HOME CONNECTION The next time you take a ride in a car, make a game of thinking of as many _ar_ words as you can.

Harcourt

Name _____

▶ **Write the word that best completes each sentence.**

friend   friends

_____

- - - - - - - - - - - - - - - - - - -

1. The two _____ go shopping.

ball   balls

_____

- - - - - - - - - - - - - - - - - - -

2. They get a bat and a _____ .

hat   hats

_____

- - - - - - - - - - - - - - - - - - -

3. They get two _____ .

girl   girls

_____

- - - - - - - - - - - - - - - - - - -

4. One _____ wants a snack.

apple   apples

_____

- - - - - - - - - - - - - - - - - - -

5. They get some red _____ to eat.

SCHOOL-HOME CONNECTION Let your child help you make a shopping list. Ask which words on the list name more than one.

Bright Ideas
Lesson 6 **13**

Harcourt

Name _____

▶ **Write the word in the box that best completes each sentence.**

says	these	always	by	people

_____

1. We _____ like to come to this shop.

_____

2. We like to look at all of _____ things.

_____

3. Lots of _____ come here.

_____

4. My friend comes _____ this shop, too.

_____

5. She _____, "Let's go there every day!"

Bright Ideas
Lesson 7

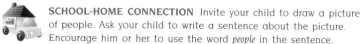

SCHOOL-HOME CONNECTION Invite your child to draw a picture of people. Ask your child to write a sentence about the picture. Encourage him or her to use the word *people* in the sentence.

Harcourt

Name ______________________________

Read the word. Circle the pictures whose names have the same vowel sound.

1. start

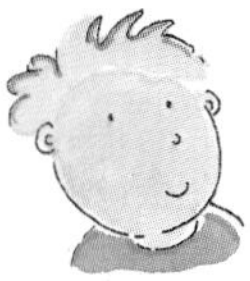

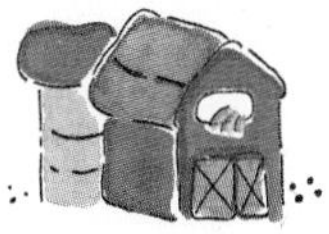

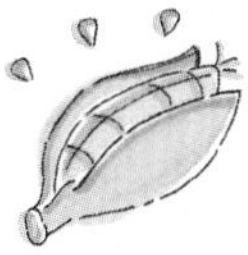

2. dark

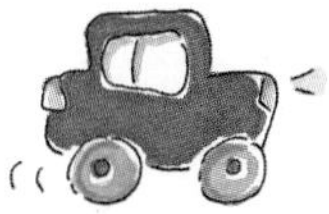

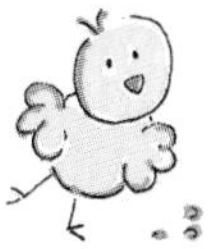

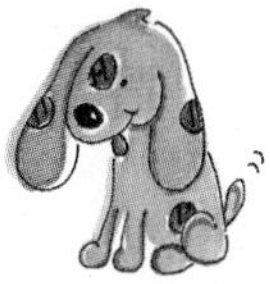

3. hard

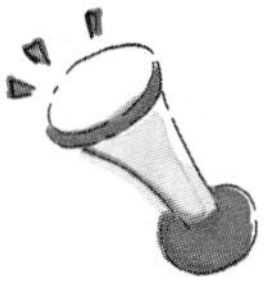

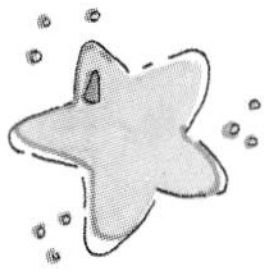

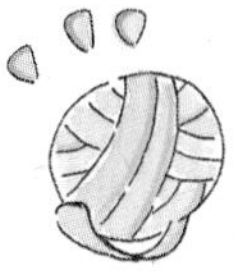

Read the sentences. Write the word that best completes each one.

farm **form**

4. The ____________________ is small.

---

barn **bark**

5. The horse snorts in the ____________________.

---

card **car**

6. The dog barks at the ____________________.

SCHOOL-HOME CONNECTION Talk with your child about the jobs of people you know. Discuss when people start their work day.

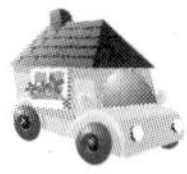

▶ **Draw pictures to show what happens during the morning, the day, and at night. Write a sentence about each picture.**

Morning

Day

Night

SCHOOL-HOME CONNECTION When you and your child shop together, talk about the names of the items on display and the way they are organized by categories.

Harcourt

▶ **Circle the word that best completes the sentence. Then write the word.**

yak

hard

yard

_____

1. Let's play in my _____.

yams

hams

slams

_____

2. We can plant some _____.

yes

yell

sell

_____

3. Don't _____ or you'll

scare the chicks.

go

too

you

_____

4. Would _____ like to come?

Yes

Mess

Nest

_____

5. _____, I would.

TRY THIS Draw a picture of your backyard. Fill it with things you'd like to play with.

SCHOOL-HOME CONNECTION Look for clothes or objects that are made from yarn.

Bright Ideas
Lesson 8   **17**

▶ **Write the word in the box that best completes each sentence.**

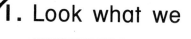

give	made	keep	make

1. Look what we
   _____
   - - - - - - - - - - - - - - -
   _____!

2. We like to
   _____
   - - - - - - - - - - - - - - -
   _____ them!

3. I'm going to
   _____
   - - - - - - - - - - - - - - -
   _____
   this to my gram.

4. I want to
   _____
   - - - - - - - - - - - - - - -
   _____
   this one at home.

TRY THIS Write about something you can make. Use the words <u>made</u> and <u>make</u>. Then draw a picture of the thing you can make.

Bright Ideas
Lesson 9

 SCHOOL-HOME CONNECTION Write the four vocabulary words on a piece of paper. Have your child read each word aloud to you. Then ask your child to practice writing the words.

Harcourt

Name _____

▶ **Circle the sentence that tells about each picture.**

1. The small dog yips and yaps.
   Yes, that is a yak.
   Len is yanking its tail.

2. The kids yell in the barn.
   The kids play with the yarn.
   The kids play in the yard.

3. Tim plays with the yarn.
   Tim has a yellow hat on.
   Tim did not put his hat on yet.

4. "Will you plant this yam?" said Mom.
   "This gift is for you," said Mom.
   "Here is your cake," said Mom.

5. The big dogs yelp.
   The fans are not here yet.
   The happy fans yell.

TRY THIS Draw a picture or design. Use only your yellow crayon and one other color.

 SCHOOL-HOME CONNECTION Say word pairs like *wet/yet*, *yes/less*, *yap/rap*, and *fell/yell*. Ask your child to say yes when you say a word that begins with y.

▶ **Write what happened in each part of the story. Use the picture clues to help you write your answers.**

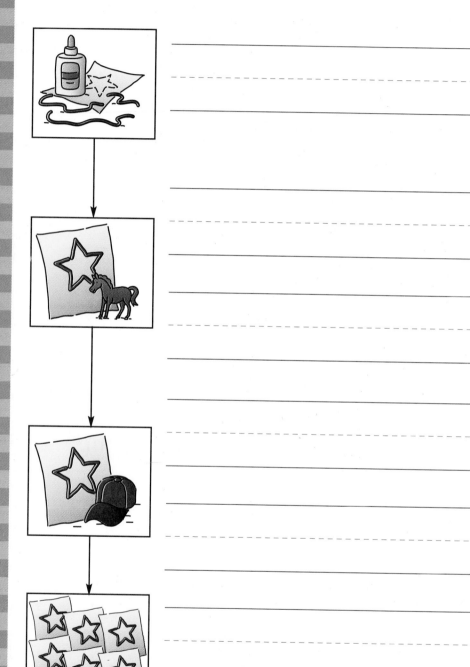

SCHOOL-HOME CONNECTION Find things in your home that were handmade by a friend or family member. Talk about why handmade gifts are special.

Harcourt

Name _____

▶ **Finish each sentence. Put together the word and the word ending above the line. Write the new word on the line.**

look + s

_____

_____

1. Nick _____ at all the stars.

want + ed

_____

_____

2. He _____ a big red star.

paint + ing

_____

_____

3. "I am _____ a red star," said

the man.

TRY THIS Write your own sentence about Nick. Use the word shout, and add the ending ed.

SCHOOL-HOME CONNECTION Ask your child to choose one of the sentences on this page and read it aloud. Discuss the ending added to the verb.

Bright Ideas
Lesson 10   21

Harcourt

Name _____

▶ **Read the story. Then finish the sentences.**

A Little Horse Is Born

One morning a little horse was born on our farm. The little horse was not in the barn. It was in the yard by a stack of corn. Dad got me up to see it. I grabbed my yarn hat and ran to the yard.

I watched as the little horse got up on its thin little legs. It made one step and then another. The mother led the little horse to the barn.

1. A little horse was

_____

- - - - - - - - - - - - - -

_____ .

2. It was by a stack of

_____

- - - - - - - - - - - - - -

_____ .

3. I grabbed my

_____

- - - - - - - - - - - - - -

_____ hat.

4. The little horse was led

_____

- - - - - - - - - - - - - -

to the _____ .

Harcourt

Name _____

▶ **Name each picture. Write the word from the box.**

| duck | bug | cup | truck | skunk | bus |

1.

_____

- - - - - - - - - - - - - - - - - -

_____

2.

_____

- - - - - - - - - - - - - - - - - -

_____

3.

_____

- - - - - - - - - - - - - - - - - -

_____

4.

_____

- - - - - - - - - - - - - - - - - -

_____

5.

_____

- - - - - - - - - - - - - - - - - -

_____

6.

_____

- - - - - - - - - - - - - - - - - -

_____

SCHOOL-HOME CONNECTION Start with the word *bug*.
Take turns replacing the initial or final letters to create
more short *u* words.

Bright Ideas
Lesson 11

23

Harcourt

▶ **Read the sentences. Write the special names and special titles.**

1. bud dunn

_____

- - - - - - - - - - - - - - - - - - -

_____

2. uncle chuck _____

_____

3. mrs. dunn _____

_____

4. dr. duff _____

_____

5. russ _____

_____

6. mr. huff _____

SCHOOL-HOME CONNECTION Help your child make a list of people he or she knows. Make sure all the names and titles begin with a capital letter.

Harcourt

Name _____

▶ **Write the word that best completes each sentence.**

takes   tell   that

1. She _____ her dog for a walk.

go   goes   gone

2. She _____ to the park.

through   three   tired

3. They can run _____ the trees.

to   takes   ten

4. She _____ her dog home.

Harcourt

🚚 **SCHOOL-HOME CONNECTION** With your child, take turns saying sentences that use the word *first*. Then have your child try to write one of the sentences.

Bright Ideas
Lesson 12   **25**

▶ **Cross out the word that is wrong.**
Write the correct word.

1. The pigs play in the

_____

m~~ad~~. _____mud_____

2. The pup is in the tab.

_____

_____

3. Dad gave
him a hog.

_____

_____

_____

4. The men pack the trick.

_____

_____

5. The friends had fin.

_____

_____

_____

6. He jumped over the
stamp.

_____

_____

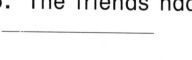

SCHOOL-HOME CONNECTION Say a sentence with one
incorrect word. Challenge your child to listen carefully,
identify the word, and say the sentence correctly.

Harcourt

Name _____

▶ **Color the animals Marco pretends to be.**

1.

2.

3.

4.

5.

6.

▶ **Write about an animal you'd like to be. Tell why.**

_____

_____

_____

_____

_____

_____

_____

SCHOOL-HOME CONNECTION Ask your child to choose an
animal and show how it moves. Guess which animal it is. Take
turns acting out and guessing other animals.

Bright Ideas
Lesson 12

Harcourt

Phonics
Consonants: /j/j,
/z/z, zz,
Digraph: /kw/qu

▶ **Read the word. Circle the pictures whose names have the same beginning sound.**

1. jazz

2. zip

3. quit

▶ **Read the sentences. Write the word that best completes each one.**

puzzle   juggle

_____

4. Have you seen this _____?

___

quit   quick

_____

5. The cheetah is very _____.

___

jug   just

_____

6. I got there _____ in time.

Harcourt

▶ **Write the word that completes each sentence.**

little   lives   let's

_____

1. What animal _____ in this shell?

about   another   answer

_____

2. We can find out _____ animals.

red   rat   read

_____

3. We can _____ some books.

even   every   end

_____

4. We can _____ look for shells.

▶ **Draw a picture to answer the question.**

5. Who lives in this house?

SCHOOL-HOME CONNECTION Write the word *lives*, and have your child read it aloud. Then ask your child, "Where do we live?" Help your child review your address, and have him or her write a sentence that begins "I *live* . . . ."

Phonics

Consonants: /j/j,
/z/z, zz,
Digraph: /kw/qu

▶ **Write a word from the box that best completes each sentence.**

jump	Zeb	quit	job	quick	jazz

1. _____ plays a horn.

2. He can play _____.

3. He does a good _____.

4. His songs are so _____!

5. They make us want to _____.

6. We don't want him to _____.

SCHOOL-HOME CONNECTION Listen to music with your child. Find a fast song and then jump and jig together.

Harcourt

Name _____

▶ **Think about the animals in the story.**
Complete the story web.

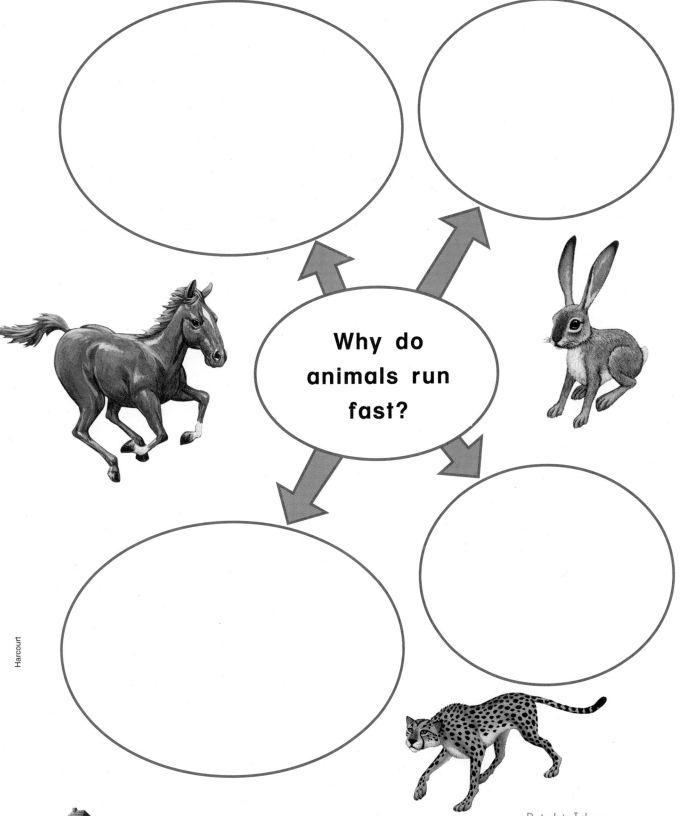

Why do animals run fast?

�

SCHOOL-HOME CONNECTION Look at the web. Together, see if
you and your child can think of other animals that are fast.

Bright Ideas
Lesson 14

31

Name _____

▶ **Write the word from the box that names each picture.**

blocks	clap	flag	plant	plum	sled

1.

_____

- - - - - - - - - - - - - -

_____

2.

_____

- - - - - - - - - - - - - -

_____

3.

_____

- - - - - - - - - - - - - -

_____

4.

_____

- - - - - - - - - - - - - -

_____

5.

_____

- - - - - - - - - - - - - -

_____

6.

_____

- - - - - - - - - - - - - -

_____

SCHOOL-HOME CONNECTION Ask your child to choose one of the pictures on this page and read the word that names the picture. Together, think of other words that begin with the same sounds.

Harcourt

Name _____

▶ **Write <u>ump</u> or <u>amp</u> to complete each sentence.**

_____
- - - - - - - - - - - - -

1. Gr _____ and I

   look for animals.

   _____
   - - - - - - - - - - - - -

2. We tr _____ through

   grass and trees.

3. We see a rabbit by an old tree

   _____
   - - - - - - - - - - - - -

   st _____ .

   _____
   - - - - - - - - - - - - -

4. We see a pl _____ robin.

   _____
   - - - - - - - - - - - - -

5. Then we c _____ and eat lunch.

   _____
   - - - - - - - - - - - - -

6. When it starts to get d _____ , we

   go home.

SCHOOL-HOME CONNECTION *Start with the word* grump.
Take turns replacing letters to create new words.

Bright Ideas
Lesson 15

33

Harcourt

▶ **Say the name of each picture. Color the pictures with names that begin with v.**

TRY THIS Where would you like to go in a van? Draw a picture and write a sentence to answer the question.

Bright Ideas
Lesson 16

 SCHOOL-HOME CONNECTION With your child, think of words, including names, that begin with *v*.

Name _____

▶ **Read each sentence. Circle the special name of a place. Then write that special name correctly.**

1. We like to walk up apple hill.

_____

- - - - - - - - - - - - - - - - - - - -

_____

2. Who got wet in pink pond?

_____

- - - - - - - - - - - - - - - - - - - -

_____

3. It's fun to play in rock park.

_____

- - - - - - - - - - - - - - - - - - - -

_____

Snack Shop

4. We can eat at snack shop.

_____

- - - - - - - - - - - - - - - - - - - -

_____

TRY THIS Write the special name of a place you like to visit. Draw a picture of that place, too.

SCHOOL-HOME CONNECTION Let your child read aloud one of the special place names. Then help your child think of the special names of other places.

Bright Ideas
Lesson 16

35

Harcourt

Name _____

▶ **Write the word that best completes
each sentence.**

what   who   way

_____

1. We are on the _____ to the park.

fend   found   fell

_____

2. We _____ a ball.

under   up   use

_____

3. It was _____ the tree.

when   way   was

_____

4. Now we are on the _____ home.

SCHOOL-HOME CONNECTION Have your child use
the words *found*, *under*, and *way* in sentences.

Harcourt

▶ **Look at each picture. Circle the word that completes the sentence. Then write the word.**

pet   vet   vest

_____

- - - - - - - - - - - - -

1. Do we have to take Puff to the _____?

Yell   Tell   Yes

_____

- - - - - - - - - - - -

2. _____, Puff does not look well.

yam   yet   van

_____

- - - - - - - - - - - - -

3. Dad can take us in the _____.

 TRY THIS Write your own sentence about Puff and the vet.
Draw a picture to go with your sentence.

SCHOOL-HOME CONNECTION Ask your child to identify and read aloud three words that begin with v. Then encourage your child to say other words that begin with the same sound.

Bright Ideas
Lesson 17   **37**

Harcourt

Name _____

▶ **Tell how Tiger's things helped Hippo on
their picnic.**

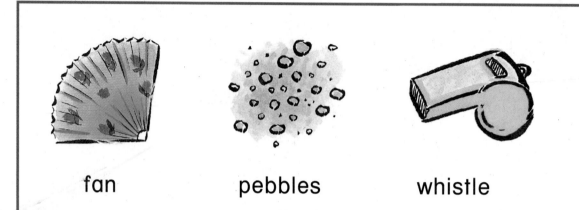

fan   pebbles   whistle

Bright Ideas
Lesson 17

SCHOOL-HOME CONNECTION Talk with your child about what
to pack for a picnic. Gather all of those things and have a
picnic together.

Harcourt

▶ **Complete each rhyme.**

1. I bet you can see my pet.

He is with the ⬚⬚⬚.

2. Today I look my best.

I have a red ⬚⬚⬚⬚.

3. Do you see that man?

He is in the ⬚⬚⬚.

▶ **Unscramble the letters siitv. Write the word.**

_____

- - - - - - - - - - - - - - - - - -

_____

SCHOOL-HOME CONNECTION Encourage your child to tell you about some of the pictures that can be named with words beginning with *v*. Then have your child practice writing the letter *v*.

Bright Ideas
Lesson 18

39

Name _____

▶ **Write 1, 2, and 3 to put the pictures in order. Then write the sentences in order.**

[ ] The robin has eggs.

[ ] The robin makes a nest.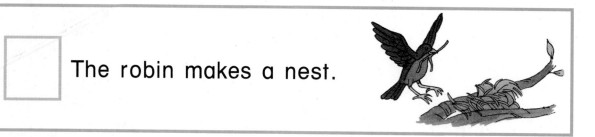

[ ] The eggs hatch.

1. _____

2. _____

3. _____

SCHOOL-HOME CONNECTION Let your child point to the pictures in order and then read the sentences in order. Ask what happened first, next, and last.

Harcourt

▶ **Write the word from the box that best completes each clue. Then draw a line to the correct animal.**

came	away	green	high

1. It can sting.

_____

- - - - - - - - - - - - - - -

I can fly _____.

_____

- - - - - - - - - - - - - - -

2. It _____ from an egg.

It will be a hen one day.

3. It can swim.

_____

- - - - - - - - - - - - - - -

It can jump _____.

_____

- - - - - - - - - - - - - - -

It is _____.

TRY THIS Write your own clues about another animal.
Use one or more of the words in the box.

SCHOOL-HOME CONNECTION Play a guessing game with your child. Give simple clues for each vocabulary word. When your child guesses the word, have him or her try to write it.

Harcourt

Name _____

Phonics

Short Vowel: /u/u
Consonants: /j/j,
/z/z, zz
Digraph: /kw/qu

▶ **Write the words where they belong in the puzzles.**

| up | sun | run | jet | jug | zipper | quilt |

Bright Ideas
Lesson 19

SCHOOL-HOME CONNECTION Talk with your child about the crossword puzzles. Ask which word begins with z. Ask your child to think of other words that begin with the same sound.

Harcourt

Name _____

▶ **Draw pictures to show some of the
things the child wonders about in the story.
Label your pictures.**

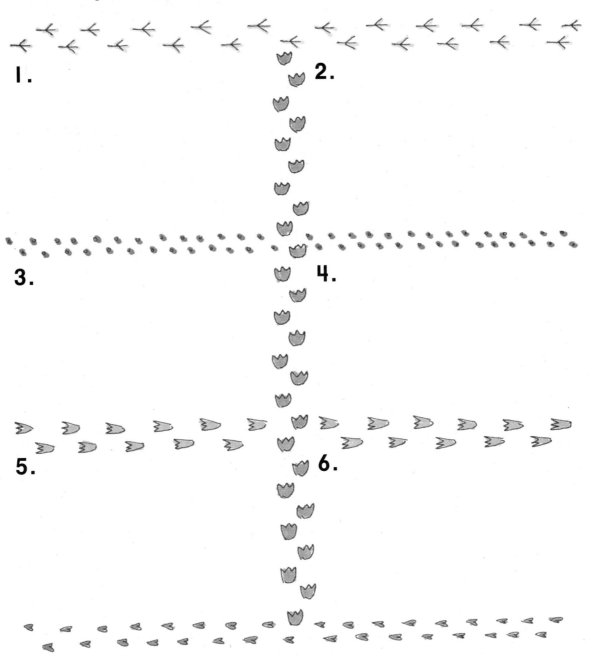

1.

2.

3.

4.

5.

6.

 **TRY
THIS** Draw a picture of something you wonder about. Write
a sentence that starts with <u>I wonder</u> to go with it.

SCHOOL-HOME CONNECTION Take a walk with your child. Look
for things to wonder about.

► **Finish each sentence. Write the contraction for the two words.**

You are

_____

- - - - - - - - - - - -

1. _____ good at jumping.

They are

_____

- - - - - - - - - - - -

2. _____ jumping very high!

I have

_____

- - - - - - - - - - - -

3. _____ jumped higher than that.

We are

_____

- - - - - - - - - - - -

4. _____ all doing our best.

 TRY THIS Use one of the following sentence starters to tell about something you have done or would like to do. I've always wanted to or We're going to.

SCHOOL-HOME CONNECTION Have your child write the contraction I've. Ask your child which two words are put together to form that contraction.

Harcourt

Name _____

► **Write the word that best completes each sentence.**

jumped   jumping

_____

1. One frog _____ into the pond.

jumps   jumping

_____

2. Two more frogs are _____ in.

look   looking

_____

3. The big dog is _____.

jumps   jumping

_____

4. The big dog _____ in.

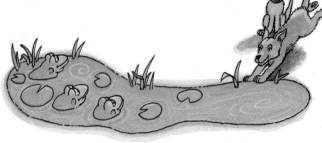

SCHOOL-HOME CONNECTION With your child, make up sentences using the words *jump, jumps, jumped,* and *jumping.* See who can make the silliest sentence.

Bright Ideas
Lesson 20   **45**

Harcourt

▶ **Write the word from the box that best completes each sentence.**

her	fur	girl	purr	bird

1. The _____ stands still.

2. She sees a little _____.

3. Here comes _____ cat.

4. She pats the cat's _____.

5. The cat starts to _____.

Name _____

▶ **Read each sentence. Circle the name of the day. Then write the name correctly.**

1. On monday we fed the pigs.

_____

- -

_____

2. We fed the ducks on wednesday.

_____

- -

_____

3. We walked the horses on thursday.

_____

- -

_____

_____

- -

4. On friday we rest! _____

TRY THIS Write a sentence about your favorite day of the week. Use the name of the day in your sentence.

SCHOOL-HOME CONNECTION With your child, use a calendar to review the names of the days of the week.

Bright Ideas
Lesson 21   **47**

Name _____

▶ **Write the word that best completes
each sentence.**

use	around	their	right

1. "I could _____

   some help here!" I cried.

2. My friends came _____ and looked.

3. "That is not the _____ box," said Jan.

4. I had to get the box without _____
   help.

TRY THIS Write a set of directions to your house. Use the
words <u>right</u> and <u>around</u>.

 SCHOOL-HOME CONNECTION Write the word *their* and have your
child read it aloud. Take turns making up sentences using this
word. Together, choose one of the sentences and write it down.

Harcourt

Name _____

▶ **Write the word from the box that best completes each sentence.**

first	purple	birds	ever	turns

_____

1. Five _____ are standing here.

2. They will take _____.

3. The _____ one is by the birdbath.

4. Will she _____ fly?

5. One bird is _____.

TRY THIS Write your own sentence about being first. Draw a picture to go with your sentence.

SCHOOL-HOME CONNECTION Encourage your child to suggest words that rhyme with *her*.

Bright Ideas
Lesson 22   49

Harcourt

▶ **Look at the pictures that show how to make a turnip pie. Tell the story by writing the sentences for the pictures.**

First, Digger Pig

_____

- -

_____

Then, Digger Pig

_____

- -

_____

Next, Digger Pig

_____

- -

_____

Last, Digger Pig

_____

- -

_____

TRY THIS Would you share the turnip pie with your friends? Write a few sentences to tell why or why not.

SCHOOL-HOME CONNECTION Let your child help you prepare a simple food. Talk about the steps as you follow the directions.

Harcourt

Name _____

▶ **Look at each picture. Circle the word that completes the sentence. Then write the word.**

hunch   lunch   match

_____

1. What did you bring for _____?

such   crunch   bunch

_____

2. I have a _____ of these.

much   such   switch

_____

3. Do you want to _____?

Stitch   Catch   Batch

_____

4. _____ this!

TRY THIS Write a sentence with the word <u>much</u>. Draw a picture to go with your sentence.

SCHOOL-HOME CONNECTION With your child, list several things that are found in the *kitchen*.

Bright Ideas
Lesson 23   51

Harcourt

Name _____

▶ **Look at the pictures and read the questions. Then write a sentence to answer each question.**

1. What does Stan do first?

_____

- -

_____

2. What does he do next?

_____

- -

_____

3. What does Stan do last?

_____

- -

_____

SCHOOL-HOME CONNECTION Let your child tell you the story in the pictures on this page. Ask, "Why wouldn't the story make sense if you mixed up the order?"

Harcourt

Name _____

▶ **Write the word in the box that best completes each sentence.**

open	house	outside	book

1. Robert left the _____.

2. He went _____.

3. Robert saw a _____ on the grass.

4. He will _____ it.

▶ **What will he see in the book? Draw your answer.**

SCHOOL-HOME CONNECTION Encourage your child to talk about books he or she wants to read or listen to. Help your child write a list of interesting titles. Have your child write a title for the list.

Harcourt

Name _____

▶ **Look at the picture. Choose a word from the box that best completes each sentence.**

girl	dirt	fern	Her	curb

_____
- - - - - - - - - - - -

1. The _____ is planting.

_____
- - - - - - - - - - - -

2. She is planting a _____.

_____
- - - - - - - - - - - -

3. She is sitting on the _____.

_____   _____
- - - - - - - - - -   - - - - - - - - - -

4. _____ hands are in the _____.

SCHOOL-HOME CONNECTION Write the word *hurt*, and let your child read it aloud. Together, think of other words that have the *ur* sound.

Name _____

▶ **Draw a picture of a Snerd. Then use words in the box to complete the sentences.**

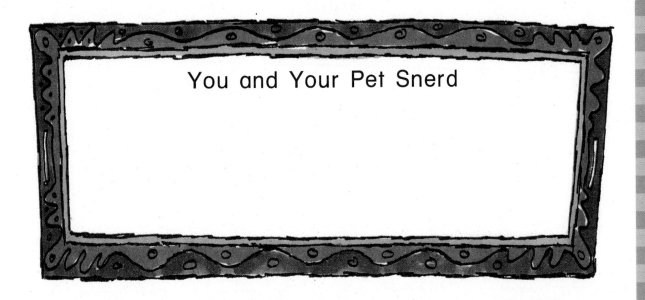

You and Your Pet Snerd

| sweet | chirp | fur | smart |

1. Snerds are very _____.

2. A happy Snerd will _____.

3. It has long purple _____.

4. Give it _____ snacks to eat.

SCHOOL-HOME CONNECTION Make up an imaginary pet with your child. Let your child draw its picture. Talk about how to care for it.

Bright Ideas
Lesson 24

55

Harcourt

Name _____

▶ **Finish each sentence. Add <u>er</u> or <u>est</u> to the word above the line.**

small
_____

- - - - - - - - - - - - - - -

1. The fox is _____ than I am.

high
_____

- - - - - - - - - - - - - - -

2. But he can jump _____ than I can.

fast
_____

- - - - - - - - - - - - - - -

3. The ostrich is the _____ animal.

smart
_____

- - - - - - - - - - - - - - -

4. I am the _____ of all.

Bright Ideas
Lesson 25

SCHOOL-HOME CONNECTION Choose an object in your home. Ask your child to find something that is *bigger* than the object. Continue the game by having your child find other objects that are bigger in your home.

Harcourt

▶ **Circle the word that completes each sentence. Then write the word.**

class
clip

_____
- - - - - - - - - -

1. Our _____ knows about animals. **cluck**

---

clock
flick

_____
- - - - - - - - - -

2. We saw a _____ of birds. **flock**

---

melt
help

_____
- - - - - - - - - -

3. I think the birds need _____. **gold**

---

clan
plan

_____
- - - - - - - - - -

4. We _____ to find out about fish. **play**

TRY THIS What do you plan to find out about? Write one or two sentences. If you want, draw a picture, too.

SCHOOL-HOME CONNECTION Ask your child to write or spell the word *flat*. Then ask your child to think of other words that begin with *fl*.

Bright Ideas
Lesson 25   **57**

Harcourt

▶ **Write the word from the box that best completes each sentence.**

goat	grow	slow	mow

I. Why does the grass

_____

- - - - - - - - - - - - - -

_____ so fast?

_____

- - - - - - - - - - - - - -

2. I wish it would _____ down.

_____

- - - - - - - - - - - - - -

3. I don't like to _____ the grass.

_____

- - - - - - - - - - - - - -

4. Would a _____

eat the grass?

 TRY THIS Write a sentence with the word <u>boat</u>. Draw a picture to go with your sentence.

SCHOOL-HOME CONNECTION Encourage your child to suggest words that have the same sound you hear in the middle of the word *boat*.

Harcourt

Name _____

▶ **Read each sentence. Circle the name of the month. Then write the name correctly.**

1. Is it cold in january?

_____

- -

_____

2. Do foxes put on vests in february?

_____

- -

_____

3. Do they take off their hats in april?

_____

- -

_____

4. Is august too hot?

_____

- -

_____

TRY THIS Write a sentence about the month you like best. Draw a picture to go with your sentence.

SCHOOL-HOME CONNECTION With your child, use a calendar to review the names of the months. Then help your child write the name of his or her birthday month.

Bright Ideas
Lesson 26

Harcourt

Name _____

▶ **Finish the story. Write the word in the box that best completes each sentence.**

kind	soon	door

The bell rang. I opened the

_____

- - - - - - - - - - - - - - -

_____ .

Ted was there. "Hello," he said.

"Come in," I said. "Would you like to have lunch?"

_____

- - - - - - - - - - - -

"What _____ of lunch are you going
to have?"

My mom said, "We are having soup and fish sticks.

_____

- - - - - - - - - - - -

We are going to eat _____ ."

_____

- - - - - - - - - - - -

"How _____ of you to ask," said Ted.
"Thank you."

 TRY THIS Write a story about your favorite kind of food. Draw
a picture to go with it.

 SCHOOL-HOME CONNECTION Write each vocabulary word on
two slips of paper. Place the slips face down. With your child,
turn over two slips at a time and read them aloud. If they are
the same, set them aside. If not, turn them down again.

Harcourt

Name _____

▶ **Choose the correct column for each word in the box. Write the word under <u>boat</u> or <u>crow</u>.**

| snow | coat | road | soap | bowl | yellow |

boat   **crow**

_____   _____

- - - - - - - - - - - - - - -   - - - - - - - - - - - - - - -

_____   _____

- - - - - - - - - - - - - - -   - - - - - - - - - - - - - - -

_____   _____

- - - - - - - - - - - - - - -   - - - - - - - - - - - - - - -

_____   _____

- - - - - - - - - - - - - - -   - - - - - - - - - - - - - - -

Harcourt

SCHOOL-HOME CONNECTION With your child, write a short poem with words that contain long vowel /ō/ spelled *oa* and *ow*.

Name _____

▶ **Write what happened in each part of the story. Use the picture clues to help you write your answers.**

First, Fox asks Stork

_____

- -

_____

Then, Stork

_____

- -

_____

Next, Fox

_____

- -

_____

At the end, Fox knows

_____

- -

_____

SCHOOL-HOME CONNECTION Ask your child to tell you the story. Help your child think of kind things to do for family members and friends.

Harcourt

Name _____

▶ **Read the letter. Write the word that best completes each sentence.**

Dear Meg,

more   morning
_____

I had fun outside this _____.

car   corn
_____

My dad and I washed the _____.

snow   soap
_____

The _____ got on my dog. It

snow   show
_____

looked like _____! You can help

next time!

Your friend,
Margaret

 SCHOOL-HOME CONNECTION Have your child point out the word *snow* on this page. With your child, take turns making up other sentences using the word *snow*.

Bright Ideas
Lesson 28   **63**

Name _____

▶ **Read the three paragraphs. Number them in story order. Write a title for the story.**

_____

- -

_____

[ ] At last they came to the top. "Oh, good," cried Stork. "We are here!" They jumped onto the sled. Down they went. "What a ride!" shouted Rabbit and Stork.

[ ] Rabbit and Stork walked and walked up the hill. It was a very big hill. They felt tired.

[ ] Rabbit wanted to go sledding. He called Stork and said, "Meet me at the hill. Bring your sled."

SCHOOL-HOME CONNECTION Let your child tell you what happened first, next, and last in the story about Rabbit and Stork. Then have them draw a picture that tells what happens next.

Harcourt

Name _____

▶ **Write the word that best completes each sentence.**

because   any

_____

- - - - - - - - - - - - - - - -

1. I can jump _____

I am a kangaroo.

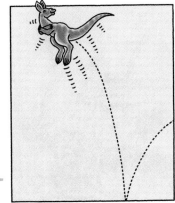

because   any

_____

- - - - - - - - - - - - - - - -

2. Can you jump _____ higher?

because   any

_____

- - - - - - - - - - - - - - - -

3. Yes, I will _____

I am big and strong.

because   any

_____

- - - - - - - - - - - - - - - -

4. Let's see if you can jump _____

higher.

Harcourt

SCHOOL-HOME CONNECTION Write a short poem with your child using the word *because.* Have your child dictate a sentence about something he or she likes to do. Add *because* to the sentence, and have your child add the reasons he or she likes the activity.

Name _____

▶ **Number the sentences to show the order in which they happened.**

Baby Joey wins. _____

The Boastful Kangaroo brags. _____

The tree cannot jump. _____

Baby Joey jumps. _____

▶ **Tell the story by writing the sentences in order.**

_____

_____

_____

_____

_____

_____

_____

_____

_____

_____

Harcourt

SCHOOL-HOME CONNECTION Ask your child to tell you about
The Very Boastful Kangaroo. Work together to play Baby Joey's trick
on a friend or family member.

Name _____

▶ **Finish each sentence. Put together the word and the word ending above the line. Write that new word on the line.**

play + ing

_____

- - - - - - - - - - - - - - - - - - - -

1. The friends are _____ on the beach.

pick + ing

_____

- - - - - - - - - - - - - - - - - - - -

2. Dan is _____ up shells.

help + ed

_____

- - - - - - - - - - - - - - - - - - - -

3. At first Carmen _____ Dan.

run + s

_____

- - - - - - - - - - - - - - - - - - - -

4. Her dog _____ in the sand.

Harcourt

SCHOOL-HOME CONNECTION With your child, talk about things you enjoy doing together. Try to use the words *played* and *playing* in your conversation.

▶ **Circle the sentence that tells about the picture.**

1. The pig sat on a cat.

The pig put on a coat.

The pigs pat the cot.

2. The pig got the bat.

The pig put on a hat.

The pig got into the boat.

3. The pig said hello to the coat.

The pig said hello to the cat.

The pig said hello to the cot.

4. A goat ran up to the cat.

A goat ran up the tree.

A coat was on the cat.

5. The goat got into the boat.

The goat got onto the cot.

The cat got into the boat.

Harcourt

SCHOOL-HOME CONNECTION Choose one of the pictures, and ask your child to read all three sentence choices. Encourage your child to tell how he or she identified the correct sentence.

Baby Chicks Hatch

1

The hen cackles again. She knows her chicks will hatch.

3

Harcourt

Some day the chicks will be hens.

8 They will hatch more chicks.

Chip! Chip! Chip!
A little chick wiggles out.

6

4

She watches over the eggs.
She does not run away.

"Cackle! Cackle!" flaps the hen.
2 Her eggs are going to hatch.

Harcourt

— Fold —　　　— Fold —

Chip! Chip! What is it?
A chick is going to hatch.

5

There is a flock of little chicks.
They hop and peck.

7

Kristen Sells Stars

1

Kristen sets up her yarn stars.

3

Fold — Fold —

Kristen sells all of her stars.
8 She is hot, tired–and very happy!

"I made them," says Kristen.
6 "All of them?" asks a woman.

4

One star is torn.
Kristen knows how to fix it.

2 The cars park at the big barn.
Lots of people are in the yard.

— Fold — — Fold —

Some people stop by.
"We like your stars."

5

"Give me two," she says. "I'll keep
one and give one away."

7

Who Am I?

1

I have wings. They help me hum along.

3

Harcourt

— Fold —　　　— Fold —

I am just a little bug. Who am I?

8

I know you have a hunch. Yes, sometimes I take a pinch.

9

Bright Ideas
Cut-out Fold-up Book
73

4

I am quick on my wings
as I fly up to the sun.

2

I am a buzzing bug. I buzz
from blossom to blossom.

— Fold —

— Fold —

5

I have six legs that
can jump and walk.

7

If I fly about you,
just say "Buzz off!"

A Jumping Green Pet

1

Harcourt

Fold

Do you want
a little bug?
It could jump
very high.

3

Yes! It's green,
and it can
jump. Now
you must
not hop
away.

8

Not even seven of
these can jump
an inch.

6

Well, some bugs are green, but that is not what I would like.

I'd like a green pet that can jump.

Fold

Fold

I found this little animal. You're going to like this green shell.

5

Here is a pet you're going to like. It came from over there.

7

Playing Outside

Harcourt

— Fold —

Who can twirl the fastest?
Who can jump the highest?

— Fold —

Let's stop twirling now. It's
time to brush off this dirt.

Oh, no! Look at the dust!
Look at the dirt!

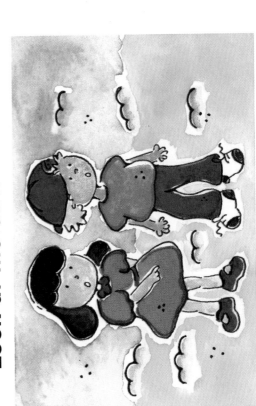

4

Turn to the right! Faster! Faster! Faster!

2

Let's twirl around!
Let's jump up and down!

Harcourt

Turn to the left!
Jump higher and higher!

5

Look at my shirt!
Look at my skirt!

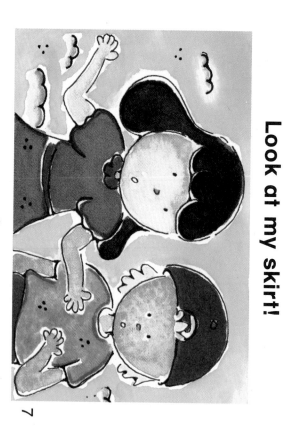

7

A Load of Stuff

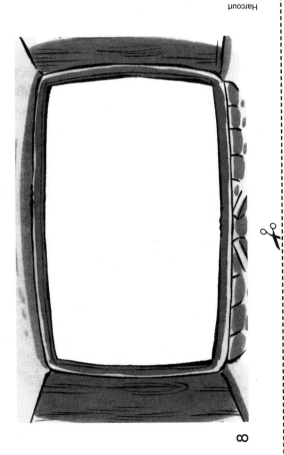

"What did you load in here?" groaned Goat. "I know we will get hungry later," said Toad.

Harcourt

Fold

Fold

Show what kinds of things were in the basket.

Goat picked up the basket, and the two friends went on.

"Let's go, Toad!" cried Goat.
"I want to go swimming!"

Goat picked up the basket
and walked down the road.
The sun glowed.

"Oh good," said Toad.
"Let's open the basket."

"This basket is too big," he said.
"Yes, but it's loaded with good
things," croaked Toad.

Fold

Fold

Harcourt

Skills and Strategies Index

Skills and Strategies Index